HEALING WILL COME

Finding Redemption, Hope, and Purpose
in the Roads of Grief and Heartache

HANNAH JOYA

Cover Painting: Dr. Danny Joya and Mary Joya
Cover design: Jbookdesigns on Fiverr
Author Image: Arielle Levy Photography

Dedication

To the remarkable woman many refer as the modern-day angel, my twin, but most importantly, the one I've been honored and blessed to call Mom. I cannot even put words into my appreciation and love for you for how you taught me by your actions what sacrificial, selfless love for others is and how you've supported, encouraged, and raised me into who I am today. I've given you many titles in my life from counselor, seamstress, personal chef, cheerleader, and "momager," but the one I truly delight in most is the joy of calling you Mom. You believed when no one else did. We held hands together in all the hard times and laughed together in all the memorable times. You're my forever-best friend. I inspire to write books because of your faith in all the late-night evening prayers. Love you so much, my model, Mom. You gave me more than the best. You are the best of the best one daughter can ever have. I owe everything to you, my number one. This book is for you.

To my dad, my inspiration, and my iron man. A few years have gone by since the moment of your first breath in heaven. The time feels as if yesterday we were taking selfies in the lobby of our hotel hangout spot. Not a day goes by when I don't look up at the starry sky and smile at you. The way you loved me for me so fiercely yet gently is what flows into my heart. You are my reason. This book is for you, too, always. Your legacy and strength pumps in my soul. I vow to keep our bond and love alive through all I do. I'll always wish my phone rang with your name on the screen. I'll always be your princess daughter, and you'll always be my iron-man dad. You were the best and coolest dad. I will forever have faith and hope until I see you again in paradise because of you. I can't wait to have another cup of coffee in heaven with you. *Mahal Kita.*

As you glance at the table in this photo, you will notice an artwork painting. My mom mixed the colors and attached the paintbrush to my dad's brace. They did this together in the nursing home court-yard. The book cover is the actual artwork of my dad's painting he did with Mom.

*A raindrop landing on your cheek
is a kiss from someone that lives in
heaven and is watching over you.*

Author unknown

Dear Friend,

I don't know about you, but I feel like we are living in the fast lane. One minute, I am holding a red paper holiday cup, drinking a white peppermint mocha, only to look down and see pink hearts on Valentine's Day, then someone is hiding color-filled eggs for us to find?! Time passes fast, but sadly, life isn't always full of great joy. Am I right, or am I right?

Life has come with countless traumatic moments, more than I wish I had to encounter. I can almost bet you also have bruised seasons that created a scar from the pain we can't put into sentences. Words cannot describe growing up as a little girl, watching my dad—my best friend—paralyzed from the neck down, the unspoken tears leading up to that dreadful day as he took his final breath. The repeated countless heartbreaks for decades, which in return ultimately caused me to question God repeatedly, *why*.

You picked up this book or someone gave this to you because you have experienced great pain and loss. You may have lost a loved one, are dealing with heartbreak, coasting through a life of disconnected nonexistence, or in a dark valley. The very moment this book landed in your hands was not by chance or accident—not even if you received this from a friend or family member. I believe God places things in your pathway for you to "find."

I believe reading a book is sacred. Time is the biggest commodity, and giving your precious time to read is stating something powerful. I want to give you a high five in taking the time to read with the lack of desire you may have had lately. Grief, loss, and heartaches can deprive the energy right out of your soul, so I applaud you and am proud of you for taking steps to move forward.

My goal is for this book to guide you to be real with yourself. I want you to begin a journey to absorb every word you read and engrave your soul with deep emotions—one where you will cry and smile and cry again. People don't talk as much about dying as they should. I mean, realistically, who wants to talk about death!? We would rather talk about the next makeup trend going viral. But I believe we need to talk about loss—in case some people have forgotten, the mortality rate is still a staggering 100 percent.

I wish sorrow and heartaches weren't part of my story. I wish I wrote about how sweet and joyous life was without the scars. But that's not the reality we live in. If you can find one person who hasn't endured pain, please email me because I'd absolutely love to meet them. In these next pages, I'll share with no filter how I went through the pain and lost everything. You will learn how I gave into the world's offer of finding happiness before realizing my faith was the only thing to allow me to be okay. I will reveal what helped me, which will hopefully inspire and help you. As a writer, my job is never to tell you how to recover because each person's healing journey is unique. So, if anyone says you must do this and that to feel a certain way, smile, and walk away and never talk to them again. Just kidding. Realize people sometimes mean no harm in their words of advice.

I tried to create an easy read of my stories and experiences to answer your "why" questions and help you better understand the purpose behind the pain so you can have peace flowing back into your life. Writing this book, I envisioned the time we could set aside and walk through the tough chapters together, coming from someone who *understands*. I desired to assemble a book without big fancy author words, but to illustrate how we are two friends meandering around the lake with a cup of coffee in our hands. We are a pair of complete strangers, becoming friends, being open to the time and space we set aside to move forward. We can be vulnerable in how we feel together and are not alone.

For most of my life, I only wanted the world's external validation, whether chasing fame, success, or relationships, but on June 13, 2018, that all changed. When something catastrophically painful happens, such as death, everything stops. My family didn't discuss our successes and awards in the days leading up to this moment. My dad didn't ask about the amount of money in his bank account. He asked for people. We talked about love. This book is about the love and relationships we build through our pain.

I can't ever bring my dad back, but I can continue to write in his honor and share everything he went through, what we went through, and never let his resilience go untold. I desire to inspire and encourage you in what we went through firsthand. My dad's journey will always be the inspiration for my books. So this book is for him. This book is for you.

In every page and chapter, my calling is to remind you gently that you are *not* alone in this season. I want to help you go through the hard questions, find the joy in chaos, feel the peace that makes no sense, and validate your doubts. Most importantly, I want to remind you again, God sees, hears, loves, and values you. Your pain has a purpose. We are here to build character over comfort.

I promise to hold the safe space for you, friend to friend. I pray you will sense the true freedom in giving yourself the time to experience the cries of your body, soul, mind, and heart. Maybe you never allowed yourself to process what you were feeling because you were so focused on your situation, but now's the time to process everything. Then, only then, will you hold the space for another friend.

You will thrive again when you don't see how you can. You are so beautifully and wonderfully made. In time, will you only know the warmth of compassion coming back into your heart.

Love, with a healing heart, your new friend,
Hannah Joya

Contents

Introduction

NOT OVER, BUT THROUGH THE PAIN

Trust in the Lord with all your heart and lean not
on your own understanding; in all your ways submit
to him, and he will make your paths straight.
Proverbs 3:5-6 NIV

*H*ow am I ever going to get over this?
I repeated those words repeatedly in my mind, at the
counselor's office, in my car, on my daily walk, to a friend,
or to my mom. The constant thought defined me. I felt broken and
that nobody understood my raw pain. *Why me?* I asked the same
thing people questioned throughout history: *if God was so good, why
is this happening?* Emotions are draining. The regrets and questions
may even put a damper on your mind all over again.

After I lost the man I couldn't live without—my hero, my
dad—I didn't think I would ever be okay. The truth is I will never
get *over* my dad not being here. You will never get over losing your
loved one or the heartache. *But you will get through your pain. I will*

get through this. Together, we will learn the difference between getting "through" rather than "over" our grief.

Let's say these words together, friend: *we will get through this.*

No Control over the New Normal

Perhaps you realize your sorrow may not disappear but diminish over time, or maybe not. Grief is different for everyone.

We have no control over when waves of emotion will come at us from many directions. But we can control how we react to the pain. We have control over what we will do now and in the future. As I write this book, I still have this longing ache in my heart.

We are all a work in progress, but we have a Father who wants to step into our lives to comfort and guide us toward a peace-filled life with no room for worries or time for anxiety. And if you haven't heard yet, having peace is possible!

You holding this book now shows you are in a readiness state. You're ready to move forward toward the life God called you to live—a life where wounds become beautiful scars. Scars represent we lived; pain represents love, and love represents hope.

In these pages, you will realize and acknowledge the truth about this new life after grief. The process is messy hard and something we wish we could erase. We are about to enter a healing journey. The promise of having joy again won't bring your loved one or my dad back. Our restoration won't bring back the years detrimental relationships stole. But you can expect to find a great sense of hope again, which is the only thing that comforts me and I believe will be the most powerful form of comfort for you.

Together, you and I will not get over our distress today. We will get through the pain, but with time. The bigger your love for your missing person, the bigger the hurt, and the bigger the hope. To continue forward, we must ground in our souls the firm foundation of God's therapeutic hands, ready to restore us to who He designed us to be. He offers us peace flowing like a cloud stream in the golden hour sunset. We can have serenity singing a song only our hearts can hear and enjoy the affirmations through the natural breeze that only we know is the love we needed to feel.

You might be thinking … *"Um, Hannah. I haven't lost anyone. So this book is not for me."*

Maybe your entire life you've believed you were such a failure to your family, so you work tirelessly at a career to prove them wrong. It could be your sorrow means processing the hurtful words from your ex, who left your life but not your heart. Or possibly, your torment is constantly comparing your life to others through the social media lens. Perhaps you no longer have an identity after the tremendous loss and pain. There is a word for all of that. We call that grief, which isn't just loss of a person, but anything that scratches on your heart.

I want to tell you, friend to friend, your feelings are all valuable. I'm so sorry you are going through those emotions. But let me remind you right now, you are not your thoughts. Your emotions and thoughts may not always be right 98 percent of the time, but you're hurting, which is real. Together, we will break things down and process the hurts you've endured through the unbearable.

We will travel together through losing a loved one and talk about how when the funeral is over, the visitors stopped checking in on you, and the text messages fade. Together, we will cry about losing special moments, heartaches, and all the "blah" ordinary days. We will share the real ugly breakups, and the "it's not you, it's me, you need to move on" moments where the person you thought was your forever has carried on. You left messages and noticed they were "seen" or "delivered" with no response. This book is about those feelings of desperation and all the in-between moments.

If you encountered any rollercoaster-drop stomach gut-wrenching moment in your life, you will benefit from our journey together. You wish a season of revival and restoration could come into place. Well, you're ready. Your time is now. Affirm to yourself right now the intention and resilience to step boldly into a new chapter of your life. The moments of late-night tears, car screams, deleting old photos, crying into heaven, or the journals with teary-eyed mascara drip can only last for a night, but be encouraged—hope comes in the morning.

Shining the Light in the Ocean

I'm excited about what's coming for you, friend. I know the past pain or even present stresses will serve as a test and ultimately become your testimony. You'll smile again one day, sooner than you expected. And you will have joy again and be okay to be by yourself, eating a smart pop with a hallmark movie, knowing your loved one is in heaven. Will you cry again? Yes, of course.... tbh (to be honest, I just did). One day, you'll genuinely smile again—not a let-me-pretend-to-be-happy smile, but a smile that truly came from the heart. If I can get through my deepest bottomless-ocean dark days, you can too.

Repeat gently while you hold your hand to your heart these words with me:

- I am BOLD.
- I am courageous.
- I have a purpose.
- I am resilient.
- I am hurting, but I will get through my pain.
- I am strong.

Now take a deep breath and pray this:

> I pray, Father, You will fill my heart with love, joy, and peace. I pray You will touch all the hurts, trauma, and sorrow I've gone through and continue

to go through with Your comforting hands. You say in Your Word, You are closer than ever when I am crushed and brokenhearted. So, I'm asking You, Jesus, please be close to me. Everything now seems so impossible, so I give You my anxieties, heartache, brokenness, and worries. Shower me with Your love and remind me again of my worth. Clothe me with Your righteousness and place Your armor around my soul. I claim victory and authority in my life. You are not a spirit of fear, and fear is not from You. In Jesus' mighty name, Amen.

With so much heartache, sadness, and uncertainty in the world, sometimes the only thing you can do is surrender everything to the One who knows everything—Jesus.

I encourage you today wherever you are to embrace the not knowing; to be here, present, and grounded, and believe in yourself and know you are loved.

You have a unique purpose and calling. Embrace your emotions and step into the hurt. To heal, you must be real. For a time, let's lay aside the self-pity and comparison of where you are in life and where others seem to be. Have faith in the God who knows you best.

Owning your vulnerabilities and story makes you...you.

Commit now to begin the grieving process. Step forward on the recovery path. You may not think you are ready or even know how to begin, but remember, God sees and accepts you as you are this very second. His love will forever change you.

Now, go shine your light as best you can.

... And one day, you will tell your story of overcoming what you went through, and your testimony will be the exact song one person needs to hear. Remember, we are living for an audience of one. Nothing else. We don't need a platform or major influence. You need a story—your story—to change the life of just one. We are tourists living on earth, one day ready to check in our true home.

We are messengers to bring the good news. We can lose and find hope again and again.

Until then, we are en route. We may have to take rest stops, but as we venture into a new purposeful adventure with an open heart, the roads will lead us toward the highway to hope. I promise your journey won't be easy, but my friend, believe and see the *healing will come.*

Chapter 1

YEAH ... GOOD QUESTION

"How could you love God after losing someone you loved so much?"

"Why does God allow some people to get better and not others?"

"Why do I have to live, and the other person must die?"

"Why couldn't my dad ever walk again?"

"Why did God allow this to happen?"

These are all hard questions people frequently asked me daily. Hard... yet good questions. People ask these questions when they see a child dying from cancer, when you have a disabled loved one, when someone good dies alone, when someone was harmed at a nursing facility, or when you were supposed to be loved rather than hurt.

You Can Ask the Hard Questions

You might be asking yourself those same legit questions. Maybe you're in a season of solid faith and feeling awesome now, or you might not even understand who God is anymore. Or you rather not even want to know Him. Maybe you're one inch away from walking away from God for good.

Before I dive into these questions and what the Word says is true, let me tell you, friend to friend, I've asked God those exact questions.

I wrote my first book, *Never Goodbye*, in honor of my amazing iron-man dad. The book was a page-by-page look at my life story I wrote in the beginning stages of my grief after losing my best friend. Since the worst week of my life in 2018—the days leading to me eventually holding my dad's left hand as I watched his heart monitor drop and his breathing slow down—I still ask those same questions.

I'll give you a little snippet of what got me to where I asked the tough questions.

My dad was disabled my entire life. The only image I ever saw of him was in a wheelchair, paralyzed from his neck down. I thought having a paralyzed parent was normal. As I got older, I understood how "not normal" my dad was.

My dad studied to become a physician and passed the board exams to become an official doctor. Then BOOM! A disease called Guillain-Barré syndrome paralyzed him from the neck down. Imagine my mom's fear and doubts—raising two kids, coming from the Philippines to the United States, and not even having her driver's license. Imagine the depression my dad must've had, losing his dreams right before his eyes and having to face his wife and two children while he lost his dignity.

I questioned God why my dad couldn't get up and walk like the other dads, why he could never take me to the father-daughter dance, or even give me a piggyback ride. I always longed to run into my dad's arms, with him picking me up and twirling me around.

I was born into a Christian family, so I always knew about faith. In my young adulthood, I often asked God why He would allow my dad to be so sick and unable to walk. Why could another girl have a dad open the door at the restaurant, whereas I opened the door for mine?

We were such a loving family and helped many people, but my

one prayer was my dad could walk. God never answered me, or so I thought. The second prayer I always asked God was He would keep my dad alive so he would be present when I got married. Again, I did not get the answer I wanted.

My brother got to experience my dad walking. Then, as a young boy, he watched his healthy dad deteriorating right before him. The man who once piggybacked my brother throughout his elementary and middle school days is now someone who can no longer walk.

Why, God?

I was hurt inside, knowing my dad wasn't around for all the "big" milestone events in my adult life. I always thought growing up in a Christian home I was strong about handling the bitterness and anger toward God and why things were happening the way they were, but that would soon change.

I lost my faith and goodness in God the day my dad took his last breath.

For one week, I watched my dad go downhill. I was on the bathroom floor at the hospital, begging God to give my dad another chance, one last miracle. I passed out. My whole family accepted my dad would pass away—except for me.

My family members were my witness that I was a mess. I lost a significant amount of weight.

I wanted to burn my Bible. I threw God's Word away. I would drive to the beach and scream so loud. I cursed God. I went from the jolly bubbly girl who found so much joy to being the depressive Eeyore in the room.

People tried telling me my dad was in a better place, everything would be okay, and God loves me. All I translated from those words of comfort was a bunch of "blah, blah, blah, and a little more blah, blah." No words could bring solace amid all the mental suffering, hurt, and trauma I endured following my dad's passing. It's as if I hit the replay button in my mind over those final moments of him on that last day. Replaying what I had just witnessed. All the good memories we had for decades seemed to have been demolished by those finishing minutes.

I didn't know how I would survive such anguishing pain.

I longed to spend much more time with my dad. I still cry at least once a week. I cried because my dad was not there before and after walking into any book event, when good things happen in my life, during holidays, and while talking about my wedding and how he wouldn't be there. I cried for all the moments I was robbed from of what our future could have been. To the social media world and friends, I may look fine, posting away a meal I'm about to indulge in, but my heart aches internally, longing for him to be back. I still battle every day, wondering why God allowed all of what we went through as a family for all those decades and how things ended. I challenge Jesus almost once a week from the verse my dad kept in his email, "'For I know the plans I have for you,' declares the LORD, 'plans to prosper you and not to harm you, plans to give you a hope and future'" (Jeremiah 29:11 NIV).

I can now say I'm not there yet fully, but I am one step closer, believing to see the "why" behind all those questions. My sister friend, God did not design us to see the full plans of His promises on this side. I believe the struggle we face when grieving is the "why"—why we lost them and why they struggled. We may never get the answer we want on this side of heaven, but I promise you, every breath you take is one step closer to knowing the truth behind everything.

You best believe when we see God face to face, we will pull out our notebook full of questions. I long for the time when God will answer *all* my questions and take away all my late-night tears and sadness. On that day, you will know exactly why they suffered the way they did, and how it was never a wasted sad story.

Only Jesus...

The only reason I still have faith in God and believe He will help me use the bitterness is that I am still here today. I could never survive and go through all I did only by my human strength. No, my strength was something more—something supernatural, something only our Jesus can step in and do.

My dad's last text message to me before he passed away told me to trust God, know God loved me, and not trust my emotions. I must honor my dad even through difficulties. Remembering what he said helps me get through those times, even if the anger, bitterness, and resentfulness are all part of moving forward.

Finding the strength to keep going is an everyday battle. I am continually learning about losing someone I loved. As I stretch my faith and remember I am not alone and God is with me, I realize God tests my faith daily. And through that test, God will remind you of your purpose even when you don't believe, see, or think you do. *You have a purpose.*

You might be like me and are wondering… *Well! Hannah still doesn't answer the hard questions.* What helped me was to write those tough questions in a journal. Prepare the pages, and write all the tough emotions, the prayers that seemed to go unanswered and the wrong and trauma that was done. Keep those pages to yourself as if you're preparing to tell the first angel you see when you walk through those gates of heaven you'd like to have a coffee date with Jesus and read those tough questions aloud.

Until that day comes, keep remembering that after God answers all our questions and wipes away all those secret tears, one day in the future, you and I can read our notebooks to each other and smile, knowing our pain was all part of the grander plan.

From all our heartache and despite feeling deserted on a worn-out island, we will know with certainty we were truly never alone because Jesus was in our passenger seat with us all along. He was holding your shoulder, crying with you in that waiting room. Jesus was with you, walking down the hospital hallway, and He was there as you opened the nursing home doors. He was with you as you sat across an empty room and while walking down that wedding aisle. He was there when you heard the horrific news. He was, is, and will be here.

Trust the process, my friend. Feel the hurt and pain. Be real to God. Ask the hard questions. Let Him know what you are feeling just isn't right.

The God who loves us will most likely not answer with thunderbolts and lightning or a raging voice, but if He does, please take a pic and tag me because I would love to see such a scene. You will notice a moment when something changes, and you can say, "Hey, I'm doing okay today." Or you may smile with a sense of genuine joy, or catch yourself wanting to do the things you once loved, or even listening to an old song that once brought you so much happiness.

Keep the faith, my friend. Run the race. The season of becoming whole again is upon us.

Chapter 2

BLUE JAY

When I lost my dad, everything felt weird, as if time had stopped, but the world kept living. Everything for me turned black and white, and I couldn't see colors. I didn't hear the sounds that music played. The only sound and color I saw and heard was nothingness. My mind replayed repetitive memories—the good and bad. I reread old texts and re-watched old videos. The normal I once knew was gone, and the new normal was this nightmare.

I was so overwhelmed and numb I even wondered if God had forgotten about me, or if I was being punished. But I didn't realize then God never let me go and had me in His loving hand the whole time. He knew it would take time to process my pain, and along the way, He sent me encouragement in small ways.

Seeing Color Again

When I went to Yosemite National Park with my family a month after my dad passed, a blue jay would often visit the house where we stayed. As I mentioned, color for me was black and white. Even seeing the beautiful magnificence of Yosemite was muted. But when this bird kept approaching our balcony, he was in a way making a statement.

As I sat there with my coffee in hand, no cell service, and an anxiety-filled stomach from losing my dad and my current relationship ending because of again finding out about new infidelities, staring out at the vast beauty was all I had. This blue jay approached me with no invitation. He flew right into my mess of emotions. As the bird stood facing me, he stared. I just stared back. I wasn't sure if we were having a blink contest, but if so, I'd call our efforts a tie between us, because the lock-in stare was a little weird if you ask me. But at that point, weird is all I was thinking. The bird could have talked to me, and I probably would have talked back.

We both had this moment where nothing around us moved, this stare. My dad's favorite color was blue. So, when I looked at the bird's feathers, for the first time I saw the color blue. Every day on our trip, that blue jay arrived on the porch, and we even put bread crumbs out for him to eat while we ate dinner (and yes I know, you aren't supposed to feed the wildlife, sorry!).

When we arrived back home, a few days passed when I was sitting in the backyard staring at the black and white trees and flowers all around me. As I cried, I turned my head to the right, and sure enough, I saw another blue jay sitting on our fence. The first color I saw again was blue. I thought something was happening. Maybe God is trying to speak to me, or my dad was trying to remind me of his love. Whatever the reason, the moment sparked a movement in my heart.

God Sees Your Anguish

You have a Father God in heaven who loves you, even when you don't think He does. I won't ever make the statements: "Let go and let God" because those words made me feel as if I'm letting my pain go. I'm letting my dad go. You're almost throwing out words to bring a sense of comfort, but, for me, I needed to work through the "letting go, letting God times." That meant having those hard months where I didn't have the strength on my own or want to open the Bible and find the comfort everyone said I would find. During those times, I needed to set the boundaries and be intentional in my emotional health. I had to say no more to hurtful relationships and learn to understand the words people spoke is often them not knowing how to relate.

I had my moments, plenty of them, so that I know those over-used phrases, despite their truth, did not help me. I didn't want to hear, "God is good" when I was so deep into missing my dad, and who would want to hear the goodness of God when you don't sense His goodness? I didn't want to hear the words from others, "at least…" Friend, those thoughts do not make you a bad person or any less of who you are to Jesus. Take the time you need to go through those motions.

You see, friend, I realized no matter how black and white and a little gray our lives may look, even while we're sitting in the heaviness of sorrow, we can still find beauty. God wants to show you the world again with color in a new vision perspective. You won't be the same, life won't look the same, but He can, and He wants to bring the color back to you. He wants you to hear the newness of songs. A clean slate, if you may say. He wants you to believe our loved one's heart is still with us; they aren't gone; you didn't say goodbye but see you soon. We must see and believe in the color of life again. One day, sooner than you think, you'll look to the right and see a color you've never seen before.

Chapter 3

GOODBYE RAMEN
AND COFFEE

With so many differences in the world, I think the one common ground we can all agree on is *life is hard*. Life is rough. One day we are on a coffee high, and life is good. The next day, we are back in our room, curled in a ball, questioning our purpose.

Perhaps you are like me and have more hard days than good ones. When the hard days come, I wish I could go straight down on my knees to pray without hesitation. But the reality is I don't pray right away. I am so quick to scroll right away to forget the reality.

When I have these hard moments, I go straight to the kitchen, pull out the ramen—the spicy ramen, to be exact—whip out an egg and mix it all together for a big bowl of comfort. Oh, and I add some extra garlic, kimchi, and seaweed.

With all the hard days I've encountered, you can only imagine how many stops at the Asian market I've made. Something about soup brings a comforting bundle of love to me.

After I get in a "food coma," I would roll back into bed (rule of advice, don't lay down after you eat unless you want heartburn), sip on my fifth cup of coffee, scroll back into my twelve-hour social media day and allow my mind to wander into the wonderful perfect lives of others rather than dealing with my true emotions. Does this sound familiar to you?

Sometimes life can be like an enormous amusement park. We enter and enjoy the rides. But sometimes, all the twirling and up and down rollercoasters can get us so tired that at the end of the day, we don't give ourselves a mental break. We desperately look for a bench just to rest on. Most people latch on to their phones and scroll away, consuming way too much more information than one may need before adding and consuming unhealthy meals to further the brain funk. I could have done those things my entire life, especially with all current rough days and those ahead.

An Intentional Fight

I wasn't fully aware we needed to be intentional about fighting the good fight every day. We need to stand our ground and speak aloud every morning that God is for us. God will fight for us and defeat the demons in our minds, urging us to give up. He will help us recover and will fight the anxiety, panic attacks, and our sense of hopelessness.

If we don't, and we flow through the unhealthy habits to numb the reality or eat the junk food to fulfill something inside, we will be stuck in a cycle which brings us down even further. Behavior begins in the mind, so be resilient on getting to the root and speaking aloud the transformation and renewal of the mind which is possible. We have an enemy of the mind, working overtime to ensure your broken heart never mends.

"Be transformed by the renewing of your mind."
Romans 12:2 NIV

We need to be intentional about seeking peace, setting time aside to go for a thirty-minute wellness walk with no distractions, and logging off social media for a few days to reconnect with our lives. We need to be more concerned about what God wants in our lives rather than consuming what the next TikTok trend is. Eating healthy food for our soul, the temple of God, will make us become our best. And when we become our best, we feel our best, and when we feel our best then we can do our best.

Intentional Purpose

After finishing my first book, I knew I was called to write. When I intentionally lived my life with purpose, I felt closest to God, clearly seeing the path He was calling me to walk. I could see how God was using my pain for a purpose. God was using everything my dad, my family, and I went through to help encourage others. I gained so many new incredible relationships through that book of faith I would have never known without going through the trials.

God has been taking me to new levels. With every new level, yes, there were new devils! The enemy, Satan, hates every inch of God's power speaking to your hearts. The enemy hated how my dad's passing, the previous abusive relationships, and all the heartache I suffered in between didn't break me. Instead, not allowing my losses to be of no significance, God used all my experiences to make me stronger, more resilient, and more eager toward life. You can enjoy the same too, my sister. You can allow your past to shine a light in this world that so desperately needs a friend to relate to hearing the ways you overcame what you went through and what you did.

I needed to pep talk myself to take a workout class with a friend, not with the mentality of looking good, but so I could feel good *internally*. I threw away the spicy ramen not because I was sick of the flavor but because of how the noodles were making my body feel. I needed to cut back on the caffeine a little. These were just a few small, healthy steps toward the upward mountain on recovering.

I can still hear the wise words my "iron man" dad would say, "Trust God over your emotions and count your blessings."

I needed to know the most important thing was seeking, knowing, and desiring a relationship with Jesus. Knowing God loves me wholeheartedly is the most important thing. To do that, I needed to cut certain habits.

Okay, the truth is I ate pho noodles last night, and if you haven't eaten them, go get in your car and make the trip to get some pho noodles the next day it rains. Did I have a cup of coffee this morning? Yes. Did I delete social media last night just to re-download the app this morning? Yes, again. But here is the truth…

We are not perfect, and God knows our weaknesses and strengths. He also knows our desire for change, growth, and recovering. We alone know what we struggle with, and God alone knows the depth of your deep hurts and the uninvited trauma still lingering. The things I mentioned before were causing distractions and health issues hindering my wellbeing, ultimately causing damage to my soul as well as a bad heartburn and puffy eyes. You alone know you need to split ways with some habits today because of the damage they are causing your body and mind.

The access through social media these last years has brought upon information overload. No wonder we deal with so much anxiety and stress. You can only intake so much news and highlight reels before you overstimulate your mind. God did not design us for information overloads. How can we ever hear God's truth and receive His peace of mind when all we see is the news media 24/7? You might be thinking, "Hannah, I don't get anxiety through social media or food." But maybe you get insecure and anxious from another outlet; only you can determine and work through the necessary steps.

Community is so powerful because people bring a sense of "you are not alone" community. So here I am, with you, sister, putting my arm around your shoulder while we hurt and create new habits together. I pour into you only what helped when poured into me. So, let's do this. Let's keep walking the walk and loving our loved ones in heaven by becoming the best version of ourselves. Imagine them smiling, saying, "that's my girl."

Let's remember we never say goodbye to our special person. We will see them again. Until that day, let's give them one heck of a life to watch from above.

Chapter 4

HOLIDAY MISERY

Christmas lights. The smell of cinnamon. The coziness of candles flickering while watching Hallmark movies. Smiles about ornaments while decorating the tree. Yet, here I am ... in my room, reminiscing about the last holiday with my dad a few years back, trying so hard to remember the moments and what they were like and getting frustrated with myself that I don't recall the tiniest details.

I know my dad is in heaven. I know he sees everything happening. But, oh, how much I wish he were here to laugh and sit with me one more time.

No Timeline for Loss

Friend, I don't know what your tender heart is feeling, but sometimes we are not okay. No matter how long since your loved one passed, love and loss have no timeline. The bigger the love, the bigger the emptiness. You may think as if you are here in this unknown foreign emotion, wishing something would fill the emptiness, but nothing can fill it because they aren't with us.

Whether a milestone birthday, an anniversary, a big accomplishment, or a surprise, we all wish our special person was here. But holidays can bring many different emotions.

Holidays can be much more difficult because these are the times we were supposed to be with our loved ones, planning that special gift, vacation, or those annual photos together. Our emotions intensify because we feel so alone, like an outsider with such a sad story, but we don't want to burden anyone with our "negative Nancy" ambiance. You are not, for one second, just being negative. You are moving forward while mourning.

You are a person who loves deeply and are dealing with what a new normal is for you as your experiences mold your soul. Don't let anyone make you think you are crazy or slow in your healing. You are human, my friend, and the human thing to do is cry, cry, and cry some more. Whether your loss was ten years, five years, or even five days ago, do *not* allow the time to control how you navigate these seasons. We each have our own journey and way of handling those "inside" feelings. But owning those inside feelings—seeing them for what they are and grieving through them—is when the process continues.

God loves us and wants to step into our broken hearts, always as a "gentleman." God doesn't want to intrude in our lives and bombard us. He wants us to call His name.

For me, those first holidays, especially the first, were the most painful and stomach-wrenching—an aching for which I have no words. As a friend to a friend, I'll be open with you … every holiday was and still is difficult for me. I know, I know, not the most comforting of words but I can say now, it's no longer how I will survive and get through with the holidays mindset, but now it's how I can honor and remember my special person to include them in our new traditions. Will the pain of their absence still be there? Yes. But you can create the traditions you know would have brought a smile to their face and in return to yours.

Will We Get Through and Enjoy Life?

Many of us are in this season of grappling with our emotional turmoil together. Holidays tend to bring forth a heightened over-stimulated onset of emotions, but when you add grief on top of that, the festive day brings a wave of new feelings. Therefore, I wanted to dedicate a section to those enduring a "how do I get through this?" season.

Perhaps you're feeling this sense of triggering feelings for upcoming holidays. Or maybe it's not the holidays. Maybe you just got engaged, and although you are overjoyed, you still perceive something is missing. For a moment, you wondered how your person smiled. Perhaps instead of fearing Christmas without your person, you are facing a birthday milestone, your kid's graduation, or walking through your favorite store and remembering how you used to grab something for them. Or maybe you click on a Facebook memory to see how times used to be, and you notice how different your smile looked and remember some pure bliss you once enjoyed. You wonder, "Will I ever be like that again?" Friend, news alert, you will.

I miss my dad every day. I wonder if I'll ever grasp the conflict of "he's not here, but yet he is." Such a confusing thought. Wondering if he sees me, which I know he does, but wondering how he sees me? I wonder what they do in heaven during the holidays. I would imagine a bunch of festivals of food, lights, laughing, and dancing.

A few years have gone by since my dad passed. I still get seasons of sadness, and the holidays intensify those emotions. But I have noticed that this year I see myself smiling a little more. I feel myself being okay with saying "no" to some events and more "yeses" to spending time alone in contentment and honoring what my body is expressing, whether that means getting a massage or a facial or sitting at my favorite coffee shop.

I am more aware a deeper root resides in my hard moments, so I take the time to dig a little deeper. The night before Thanksgiving, I cried and smiled the next day … with joy. I pray aloud during those moments when I miss my dad a little more. "God, give my dad the biggest hug right now and add little tickles." When I'm eating something yummy, I pray aloud, "Dad, go enjoy a big warm, fulfilling meal." Little audible prayers like this, the whispers of prayers I know God hears. One day we'll spend the holidays again with our loved ones in heaven, and they'll remind us of all the prayers they heard and the meals they enjoyed.

Be Gentle

Be gentle with yourself. Filling your sadness with a bunch of holiday activities, fearing any time you would need to be alone can be easy to do. Be intentional with compassion. Yes, you may feel lonely, but remember you have a friend in Jesus.

Give yourself time to process everything and listen to your thoughts, and I assure you the healing will begin. Sometimes sitting on your couch with hot cocoa and watching a Christmas movie is just what you need. Some days it might be necessary to journal ... while crying aloud.

But remember, my friend, no matter how alone or forgotten you feel during this season of anguish, you are never alone. Jesus is always right there, close to all, and even more so to the brokenhearted. He can be your companion or shoulder to cry on—whatever role you need Him to become. God designed love ... God IS love. Let our Creator love you as you should be loved.

Now, go get some eggnog and blast Christmas jams—even in November—and allow that dimmed magical spark in your heart to shine ever so bright in your own special time.

Chapter 5

BYE, MOCHA, CHANEL, AND VAN

A few months ago, I endured the second hardest parting in my life: the passing of my twenty-one-year-old little furry family member, Mocha. Yup, *twenty-one*! People often asked how she survived to that age, and it was lots of love and jasmine rice... just kidding. We just loved her unconditionally. She was the mother of my other two dogs, Chase and Chanel, and wife to Chance. Mocha was also a very close comrade to my dad, who loved her tremendously.

Losing a pet brings on a whole ballpark of pain. They were your lifeline—the ones who were always there waiting for you, ready to love you always. They never talked back, expecting nothing but pure love. Pets, I believe, are God's biggest gifts to humans because He knew how this life would be so tough.

Friend, if you are dealing with the loss of a furry family member, or in the place of making those tough decisions, I'm so sorry you have to go through this. Last week I had to find an in-home pet euthanasia for one of our sweet senior pup Chanel. But to our surprise, she came out of her sickness and is doing even better than before.

But the emotional rollercoaster came flooding back in when she declined, ultimately leaving us to make yet another hard decision.

I can agree to disagree with those who say animals don't go to heaven. I believe they do. And I don't know about you, but seeing your fluffy friend running down the streets of gold with their favorite toy is one sight I'd love to imagine in heaven.

Your pain is valid when grieving your fluffy one. I would often hear stories from others about how silly they think they are when struggling over the passing or illness of their pet. Acknowledge the fact your fluffy friend was with you through it all and was always ready to love you. They comforted you in a way that brought a sense of validation and were ready to greet you the moment you walked in. Your furry friend got you outside to get some fresh air and loved unconditionally.

If you are at that place on making that final decision to send your fluffy friend home, you have to look at it like this. What is the kindest thing you can do now that would help them in the situation they are in? Are they hurting? Are they having more bad days than good? You can be the one to decide if they will have another rough day or be at peace and comfort in heaven.

If your fluffy is in heaven, and you have days where the loss is too heavy, imagine the treats and toys they adored all around them. Imagine what they would be doing right now with no leash. How fast are they running? Where would they be taking a nap?

I imagine my baby Mocha and Chanel running with my dad, skipping around my future home in heaven. And when that day comes for me to see Jesus, I dream of them both sprinting into my arms, while my dad comes for the biggest bear hug. Friends, it's hard losing a pet, but allow your pain to process while you accept, dream, and hope for what's to come.

Strength to Let Go

When we go through losing someone or a fur baby, we become a new person. Life after death does something to our souls. Sometimes, we hold on to things that remind us of our lost person, and sometimes, we need to let go so we can step into the new person we are becoming.

As I'm typing this, the AAA tow truck is out there getting my dad's van ready to tow. Not just any van, but my dad's source-of-life van. My dad's van was designed for the physically disabled and came with a pullout ramp. I can imagine driving down the street pulling into a shopping plaza, looking for the blue parking spot, seeing my dad's van there with the ramp out as if we were doing this yesterday. In my memory, I can still envision my dad outside the frozen yogurt spot we frequented. I didn't want to get rid of this van. His electric wheelchair, complete with his food crumbs and extra sources of oxygen, was still in the back of the van.

My dad passed over three years ago. During the first year and even into the second, I was so angry. Pain, helplessness, frustration, resentment, hate, fear, and hurt were just some feelings that made me often completely isolate myself, physically and emotionally. I would take offense to everything so easily, as I was hypersensitive to everything and everyone around me.

Today was so difficult and disturbing to see the tow truck taking my dad's van away. My unease was not so much from seeing the vehicle towed away, but more from the realization of him not being there. In the past, seeing the van in the driveway, imagining my dad's face in the passenger window comforted me.

I took a moment to reminisce about my dad being in the passenger window at all my high school dances, our visits to the mall, and the sharing of life and laughter. I was now seeing the truck tow the vehicle away, taking away the memories.

After the tow truck pulled away, I realized I was being bitter.

I didn't get the opportunity and time to say my "goodbyes" to my long-time van. I realize saying goodbye to a vehicle may sound like a joke, but not saying goodbye gave me a sense of emptiness, like my childhood memories were being driven away—almost even as if the reality of my dad would never come back. I didn't recognize this was one of many hindrances to regaining my peace of mind.

Holding On

Seeing the van and wheelchair—exactly where my dad would sit with his cellphone—reminded me every day my dad wasn't coming back. I was idolizing the van. I would place my hand on the vehicle every day. I would go inside when I was sad. Doing those things in the beginning was okay, but after a few years, I had to ask myself, is this helping or stalling my recovery?

Sometimes objects or things can help us move past the pain, but if those things could help someone else, let them go, bringing help to another person. Trust me when I tell you, you will enjoy even more growth, knowing you helped another person's life.

An orphanage in Ensenada, Mexico, that cares for over twenty special needs children needed that exact type of special van and electric wheelchair. A part of me didn't want to let the van go. Instead of the van consuming space in the driveway while I stalled letting go, the vehicle would now provide necessary help to others who needed assistance. My dad's source of living is now pouring into these children's lives. I envision my dad smiling at the kids in the van. I like to hope Jesus is turning on the radio to my dad's favorite song while the special kids dance it out to their next doctor's appointment.

Maybe you still have your special person's shoes at the front of the house, their clothes are still hanging in the closet, or even their phone is still sitting there. Don't get me wrong, I understand. I still have my dad's fedora hat sitting in my room with his eyeglasses, but

I can smile and sense comfort in having those items. Keeping those personal sentimental items is okay. On my ring finger, I even wear my mom and dad's wedding band.

But if those items are causing your heart to remain stagnant and even go backward, you may need to consider placing them in the hands of another family member or trusted friend if you're not ready to truly give up the special mementos just yet.

While you're going through those emotions, seeing and remembering is part of the process. If the item can go toward another life or organization to help someone, I kindly ask you to pray about how you can bless another person and allow God to speak and comfort you through what you fear. People told me to get rid of the van as if doing so was the easiest thing to say, but their words were hurtful and caused anger in me … "Oh, yeah? And why don't you give your most important item away?"

Friends, grief is hard. I'll say those words in every chapter if I can. This is one of the hardest things about losing someone: letting go of items they once owned.

I couldn't even consider letting my dad's van go for three years. If you find yourself in a similar situation, please understand the decision to release something will bring a sense of lightening your burden in due time. Then, you may feel as if your special person is still there in spirit, and even more so if that release is helping someone else.

Friend, you'll be okay.

Repeat this aloud:

"I will be okay. I am safe. I am loved. I will take time to heal, and I will be okay. God will attend to my grief. God is good when I don't feel he is. I am stepping into a new season of hope. Letting go is beautiful. The best of life is still yet to come."

Now breathe.

Chapter 6

CAPTURING THE MOMENT

Yesterday, after the church service, I was chatting with a friend. As she was mid-sentence, I remembered my father's recent passing; I wasn't ignoring what she was saying, but the thought popped into my memory. "Grief pop" is popping moments that come suddenly.

As I was in the bubble of remembering my dad, I looked over and watched my mom with a full smile, talking to a new couple at our church. The joy and glow on my mom's face was such a bright light. Her heart for loving people, as God designed her to do, was showing. Everything seemed to freeze around me, and I absorbed my mom's actions at that moment. I didn't have to grab my phone to capture the moment. I simply watched and processed what pure bliss truly was. So, thanks, Mom. Thanks for that moment, frozen in time for me to watch you in your element, appreciating the small moments, not the staged ones. Happiness is not about the good times, but the simple times.

My Remarkable Mom

In 2022, my mom spoke as one of the final nominees for Remarkable Women 2022. Remarkable Women is part of a nationwide campaign to recognize the influence women make in public policy, social progress, and quality of life and celebrate local women who inspire, lead, and forge the way for other women. Someone must enter your story and wait to see if the organization will select your remarkable woman. This program is a way to honor the women who have made significant contributions to our nation and local communities.

I submitted my mom for this for years, and the one year where I told myself I was done submitting was that year. A few months later, my mom gets a call from our hometown news station, to tell her Remarkable Women selected her. My mom almost hung up because she thought the call was a scam. Three months later, she gave a live interview of her story on national television.

I remember sitting in the waiting room with my niece waiting for my mom, biting my nails, nervous as a chicken, knowing this is LIVE TV, and thinking, wow, look at this. Now my mom is sharing her side—her story, pain, heartaches, and struggles with the world. Everything designed to break her; she in return used to make her. Owning her story. Raising two adult children, while caregiving for her husband for decades and ultimately standing loyal to her vow in sickness and in health by his side. If you'd like to watch her interview, you can google, "Mary Joya Remarkable Women 2022." I am so proud of my mom and how she did her first live interview to instill hope in the community. I'm proud of how she journeyed her way through her new normal of widowhood.

My mom found so much satisfaction in helping others. She found her restoration when she empathized and sat with hurting people. To hear and listen to the ones crying over what they went through gave her a purpose. Her spark didn't diminish because of losing her husband; her heartache reignited her zeal.

She never stopped serving her ministries and continued to lead church services at the nursing homes. She still walked the streets downtown where the homeless were. Mom continued creating crafts for those who didn't have family members and provided belongings to orphanages in Mexico. Did she have moments of deep despair?

Yes, almost every day. Did she burst into tears at a grocery store because something or someone reminded her of her husband? You bet, but she didn't allow despair to detour her.

She found the greatest joy in her pain when people who needed love surrounded her. My mom shared with me the other day how most of her life has been acts of service. She was always searching for what others needed, so walking into a store was always about what someone else would like. She didn't even remember the last time she bought something for herself. She didn't even know what she likes.

Recently, my mom visited the nursing home my dad lived in the last few years of his life. I personally cannot do that yet. Maybe in the future I can. My mom showed the strength to go back and visit our old friends who still live there. She mentioned her split-second anxiety at first, but continued walking inside. She said she smiled and hugged all her friends there and even became friends with someone new who lives there.

I see how much love my mom holds in her heart for people, despite her broken heart. No words can express my gratitude I have that God selected her to be my mom. God knew I would need a living example of someone like her. I can see the restoration taking place in my mom only three years after losing her husband. My mom takes great joy in serving others. Her biggest goal in her life is to love others by serving their needs.

Seeing firsthand how my mom's resilient strength allowed her to continue loving, serving others, and empathizing brought me encouragement. Maybe you know someone who is hurting, lost, or is enduring a heartache but don't have the energy to comfort them. But comfort is not you showing up to do all the talking. Simply showing up by being there for them is what they need. When you show up to comfort them and you walk back to your car, you may even notice a sense of comfort in yourself—that's called community.

Each Moment God Gives Us Is Special

Is anyone else asking about the day or time? Or wondering what you ate for breakfast? I mean, did you even eat breakfast?

Well, if you're like me most of the time, you are here in the present, but your mind hasn't quite caught up. You catch yourself missing the opportunity to witness the moment in person because you are on your phone putting together your Instagram stories with the right angle and perfect caption. My friends know me so well regarding this. When we are out at a restaurant and the server comes out with our food, everyone knows not to touch any food until I can adjust everything on the table to create the ideal Instagram-worthy photo. I know I'm not the only one who does this.

The benefits of "being in the moment" or taking time for yourself to reflect on your feelings are wisdom. Simply going on walks with no phone so that you can become more grounded can do wonders.

Be honest for a moment … do you really do that? Do you really step aside for a moment to be still? Do you intentionally stay away from all the social media and emails, especially first thing in the morning when your eyes are still squinting at everything?

The rush of life can make us get so caught up in what others are doing and what you're NOT doing, forgetting all the blessings you already have. The enemy will do everything in his power to cause as many distractions as possible in your life. The distractions can be through filling your schedule too full or screaming lies into your thoughts. In those moments, the evil one can use even the closest people in your lives to discourage and lie in your thoughts, making you perceive yourself as behind in life. When we are working together in this recovery process, we have to set aside intentional time to seek peace and stillness.

I believe God so graciously gave us the gift of nature for us to appreciate His vast creation to guide us back into the moment and enjoy the small things of life. Next time you're outside, look at the detailed succulents. Examine the colors on each flower, the mountains across the distance, and all the different dimensions it comes with.

Every morning, I like to bring my cup of coffee and sit outside in stillness at the sound of God's creation. I just take it all in, allowing the steam from my cup to flow into the sky as the birds chirp a charming melody. I intentionally do this to bring stillness, gratitude, and serenity to the start of the day.

Today, take a moment to live the now. Experience what's happening around you. Go hug someone you love. Go text the person who puts a smile on your face. Stop waiting for magical moments, and go create them.

Go love on your loved ones in all the big and small moments.

Chapter 7

BATTLING A BLACKBERRY

re you sometimes extra hypersensitive, like you're crying about everything? Well, that usually is me, but *not* the other day. I was the opposite. I was in this "I'm a tough girl" season, singing along with confident girl music blasting in the car and feeling so good in my skin this time around. I was ready to take on the world. *Yes! I can do this.*

So when I was at an event and a triggering moment randomly overcame me out of nowhere, and I needed to run to the bathroom and cry and scream… I'm telling you… I was off. I surprised the girl in the bathroom stall next to me, and I was even more shocked than she was. What happened to that confident Hannah? What even triggered me?

Grief Triggers

A loved one's passing isn't the only thing that triggers waves of sorrow. We can feel an onslaught of emotion through losing who we thought we'd become when the life we envisioned for ourselves is not coming through. In some ways, I feel the most whole I have ever felt in a very long time. I truly believe I'm living exactly how God intended for me to. I continuously pray every day He would remove anyone or anything that should not be part of my life, and I pray His comforting love would come into my life.

Friend, it's a constant mind battle. One day may seem like you're living the life God meant for you to live. Then, one comment from a friend or coworker or one commercial will ignite everything that causes your insecurity to come spiraling out.

You must be intentional, even praying aloud, to rid your mind of this spirit of discouragement and any negative spirit causing chaos. You feel as if your life is a collection of sad memories, and everyone else has their life together except you. Even after my premier book, I got so involved with progressing that I never took the time to take a breather.

A key point was a triggering moment, which brought my trauma back up. You can be fine one moment, and then boom. You're not okay. Triggers. As much as I dislike triggers, a triggering moment is a way for our hearts to align with our emotions. "Emotional triggers, also called mental health triggers or psychological triggers, are things (e.g. memories, objects, or people) that spark intense negative emotions. This change in emotions can be abrupt, and in most cases, it will feel more severe than what the trigger would logically call for."[1]

Triggers are like a wound reopening and not having the chance to get better. Experiences are reminders of old hurtful events or emotions. Triggers may feel like our body engine starts and automatically sets us up on the flight, freeze, or fight mode. You have this extra adrenaline going off the charts. I have heard that the stress hormones like cortisol go throughout our brains and bodies.

"Please be advised this may trigger" or even be a "trigger warning." That may look like a familiar statement before watching a video or the news. Seems to be we are seeing or hearing that statement more and more in today's world. But those words don't hit you right away. When that trigger catches up, the emotional throbbing comes right back out. Then we suffer through the over-hypersensitive, crying-out-loud, not-acting-like-yourself, and having to run out the door and hide-in-your-car type of cry. The type of cry that makes you lose control. There is no timeline for triggers when heaviness or severe heartache rears their ugly heads.

Deal with Those Triggers

I'm not a psychologist, PhD, or masters' graduate, but I am a trauma, grief, and heartbreak survivor who still is healing. I can speak with confidence that triggers come whether your loss is recent or several years have passed. A trigger hitting you is not a matter of if, because they will, but more when they do. Dealing with them is hard whenever they hit. Very hard. I will step alongside you in these triggering moments to assure you that you aren't alone. You're not overreacting; you simply are crying out the deep internal hurts.

First, you must sit with this trigger, recognize it, and identify when you changed from being okay to not okay. Then determine your feeling. Name the problem aloud. Are you experiencing shame, depression, anxiety, fear, hopelessness, or anger? After you do that, try to understand why that trigger affects you so much. Was there a specific place and time something happened like this? Familiar feeling? Childhood memory?

Once you go through that cycle of identifying your triggers, you can move to the self-care stage of doing what helps regulate you back to peace.

For me, that means going outside and taking short inhales and longer exhales, knowing I am safe while working through my triggers. Journaling my emotions of what exactly I'm feeling and letting myself reflect, and listening to my triggers without judgment is also therapeutic for me. I just need to focus on giving myself the compassion I am crying out for.

An Unexpected Trigger

There used to be a device called BlackBerry… an odd-looking square phone to call people. I'm not even sure the companies run BlackBerries anymore, but I drove by what looked like the corporate building unless the fruit has its own building. Well, one person owned a BlackBerry device—my dad. Before you ask, well, wasn't your dad paralyzed? Yes, from his neck down, but he could slowly yet surely manage his BlackBerry phone.

After my moment of triggering cries, I was driving home from that event in complete exhaustion. Friend, let me tell you, your tiredness after an episode of abrupt cries is normal. Being drained to the point of wanting to lie down after that emotional tidal wave and process your thoughts is okay.

So when I was driving home, I looked out the side window and saw this building with the word "BlackBerry." The moment I saw those words, I recalled the day my dad owned that phone. I had this rush of affirmation. A sense my dad, in his own special way, was reminding me he sees me and my hurt and loves me.

I then realized the trigger was seeing a certain person who looked like a nurse on the day my dad took his last breath. I then saw daughters and dads hanging out all morning, so a combination of all that brought forth the trigger. The emotion was anger and hurt.

But after seeing the BlackBerry building, everything seemed to be okay again. Did seeing the building remove the memory? No. But did I go through the memory with sadness and a sense of moving forward? Yes. Could I unlock my white tense knuckles sitting on my lap? Yes. Was my tense neck and shoulders able to drop? Yes.

You see, friend, that is what we call triggers in a nutshell for you. We have those small or big moments more often than we like. Even though no exact order exists, grief stages vary for everyone. In the beginning, I battled with a deep, daunting sadness, or what some would call depression. I also had a mix of emotions that made no sense. You then battle, denying the problem or hurt isn't happening. Grief is an arena of mixed emotions fighting back and forth. In the beginning, your brain can't keep up as you are still in a shock state.

Triggers will cause you to remember certain details, and they may not always be the same details. I remember laying in my bed and watching my phone ring and not moving or never turning on my car radio while driving, listening to pure quiet. I recall bringing balloons to the hospital on his last days, where my dad would celebrate his birthday, so when he woke from a coma, we would have a party, but I couldn't accept the reality he would not be waking up.

I don't think anyone processes the reality, even after hearing the words spoken to others. We sometimes stand there listening, looking, but not looking, if you understand what I mean. You're in this stargaze moment, looking right through them, daydreaming about a bunch of nothing. You won't be able to process what happened until a few weeks or even years pass. With processing, these triggers come.

Friend, I am so sorry you have to encounter these triggers. The effects are so hard, and I wish you never have to go through them. But I'm learning to embrace these moments instead of running from, ignoring, or numbing them to do whatever I can to not have them. I must learn to recognize why the trigger is hurting me and see where the anxiety is navigating through my body while praying God will soothe me from the trauma.

Sister, let me tell you, God can and will ease those triggers, and you have got to keep giving your tender heart to Him. Almost imagine grasping and physically throwing that trigger in the sky. I would often have these moments where I would close my eyes and go through the memory—the sound, words, and scent. I would place those things in my hands and physically throw that memory in the sky to release that unresolved pain to the One above who knows how to handle my hurts so much better than I do.

Feel What You Need To

I am not forgetting. Did you catch how I processed and went through the pain? I allowed my body to feel what was necessary. I showed no judgment to myself, I allowed the realness to come, and I gave everything to Jesus. Giving our sorrow over to the Lord was as if our inner child has so many tears and trauma to cry out that these triggers are a way to process them in a better way.

Anguish and sadness don't just vanish, but we can learn a healthier way to go through them, but that is so much easier to say than do. Believe me, I can attest to that. The only way I could go through these triggering moments was to see the light at the end of these times and in going through them from a more beneficial perspective.

Believe again, friend, the best version of you will be the strongest. You've overcome a whole ton of heartache. Grief isn't for the faint of heart. No one will understand the pain or love for your person. Only you know the love you have for them. The tears you shed aren't meant to be shamed. The more tears you have simply mean the bigger the love. All the tears represent all the love left you wanted to give still.

I remembered my dad when I saw that building. Look around you and search for the love your person is speaking. Whether a breeze, sunset, sound, song, or the smell of a home-cooked meal, whatever brings your heart peace in knowing they are still in your soul. Search for those times or watch them come before your eyes. Our restoration is all around us. We must seek, find, and seek again.

Chapter 8

PAST. PRESENT. FUTURE.

Reliving the past. Being numb to the present. Grieving the moments for the future. Sometimes for me, life feels like I am constantly coasting along with this heaviness in my chest.

Our memories of life in the past can consume us so much that we miss the "good ole' times," which even include the frustrating hospital visits and arguments. We can fill our minds so full with the past that we don't sense the present moment, leaving us not looking toward the future.

The present often becomes a distant stare into the sky as our thoughts drift back. Then, the moments we expect to come into our future seem dreadful while knowing we should be joyful. But, knowing our loved one is gone, how can we allow ourselves to be in such a state of joyfulness? How can we be excited about all the big events our future holds?

Mourning Is Grueling

Friend, grief and trauma are exhausting. Just reading about sorrow can become tiring. The many emotions that show up and fade away are overwhelming. This road to becoming whole again can be demanding if you're not used to the stillness and work of peace.

That's why we call the road a journey. We go backward; we stay stagnant, and sometimes, we don't see any progress, but every effort, prayer, and cry of desperation is all part of the process. Be kind and soft to your soul with compassion for this change of life. What may feel like going backward is your heart opening wounds you may not have processed during that time of life.

Loss and grief aren't always about the absence of our loved one's presence but a longing for what our life used to be when we see those old photos and text messages. You see the age difference, the younger youthful "you" in the photos with your beloved absent person, which causes even more anguish knowing more time has gone by without them. When you get exciting news or a big event is coming up, the first person you want to tell isn't there to hear or see you … feelings that add to your season of pain. It becomes this feeling of constantly searching for them in a crowd.

I used to love celebrating my dad's birthday. Now, every year he isn't here on his birthday is a reminder I'll never watch him grow old. Learning to change certain celebrations is part of grieving. One year, you may be happy and celebrate with their favorite food, and maybe the next year you want to lie in bed and give your body the emotional rest you crave. Or maybe the present reminds you of a certain place you went together that brought a bunch of triggering traumas that come with hurt.

We must learn to manage those moments and dig to the deep root of what and how they make us feel. Sense where the ache is coming on your body, place your hand over the area, and pray God will send a rush of healing nerves to that spot.

Friend, the enemy wants your mind stuck in the cycle of "your life will never get better" and "your best days were in the past." The enemy wants you to forget the present and dread the future. But God wants the opposite.

Yes, You Can Look to the Future

God designed life on earth never to satisfy us fully. I believe that decision happened in the Garden of Eden. If we were to have true satisfaction here, why would we ever want to leave? God did not design the things of this earth to fulfill our hearts completely; that is saved for our ultimate paradise, heaven. I believe we will always have a longing in our hearts for more. You need the Holy Spirit's power to give you a satisfied contentment. No human being or procession can ever bring the ultimate peace our broken heart desires.

God wants your full and undivided attention, not staying in a constant run-around process. The only way to contentment and healing is through Him. So, by genuinely seeking Him for comfort and believing by faith in His time, we will have the peace we need.

No matter how successful we are or how many achievements and awards we receive, we will always want something more because God designed and created our soul for eternity. Every day we live, we are stepping closer and closer to the time in heaven of happiness forever and ever.

Are there other ways to aid this recovery process? Of course. Take time to journal your feelings, go on thirty-minute wellness walks (cell phone free), say, "No" to those activities you know can cause hurt, be intentional about meeting with a friend for coffee, and say, "Yes" to a benign new adventure. It's crucial to understand as well that not everyone will know how to support you as you learn to re-navigate life. That's why it's important when you are hurting to surround yourself with people who speak life and encouragement.

I promise you, friend, I know how cliché "The best is yet to come" sounds. But those words are true because heaven is our ultimate destination. We are here on earth for such a short, fast moment because heaven is eternal. Reflect on how fast this year is passing. Every year seems to fly.

We have the choice today. Do we want to get bitter, or do we want to get better? We can choose to make the most of what we have. Do we have to be happy all the time? No. Happiness and distress can fit together; we call this "being human."

This moment ... this day ... can be a time for you to lie down. Give yourself a moment to cry. There is no right or wrong ways to process what you're feeling. Be real with our Lord. We need to allow our hurts, anxieties, and heart-wrenching cries to be heard. Tell God exactly how you feel. Yes, He already knows, but He wants you to tell Him ... to rely on Him. Lean back, and allow the serenity flow to move into your soul, washing and slowly dissolving all the trauma from your past and present memories so you can have this peace in place for now and into the future.

Chapter 9

STARS SHINE BRIGHTER IN THE DARK

living on earth, we carry a passport that says, "Citizen of Heaven." When we enter heaven, the words change to "Resident of Heaven."

Sometimes, I think living on earth gets so familiar and comfortable we believe this is our forever home. We invest so much in our retirement, stocks, and dream home, and our Pinterest board is picture perfect. But how much are we investing in our eternal home, heaven? Heaven will last much longer than this old earth and longer than we can imagine… and time is flying.

Life Is Racing toward Our Future

I walked into a big box variety store on January 2, and everything was already about Valentine's Day! The world is going at warp speed. We still have Thanksgiving décor up, and this is January! Looking up, it seems we are on the next holiday.

I don't have any children yet, but all my friends who are new moms say the same thing about their kids, "They grew up so fast."

My mom told me she remembers, as if just yesterday, she was dressing me up. Here I am, driving her to her doctor's appointments.

Friends, we never know when our time on earth will end. Our end here could be tomorrow or next year. If you knew the dates and length of your life, you would live and love every moment as if each were the last. You would forget about all the future needless minor arguments. You would carry a lighter load and love your life more.

The sad truth is a celebration of life—a funeral—is often the only time we remember how short life is. We may remember how precious people are and how quick their life can end. Yet we think we're immortal, and other people pass into heaven, never us. A death doesn't seem real… but we continue seeing the posts from people, "life is too short; hug your loved ones tighter."

God designed our minds to grasp so much about the future and heaven. The Bible gives us glimpses of heaven and talks about our mansions, feasts, and reuniting with our loved ones. Yet, we still do not have enough information for heaven to be real to us. Heaven seems like a magical, made-up place because our eternal home is more awesome and wondrous than we can imagine. God tells us we cannot imagine what will be in heaven.

My mom has her special talk about heaven daily, which I love to hear. I think the older we get when we have a loved one go there, the more we focus on what our loved person is doing in heaven. We have more desire to learn about heaven when we know someone living there.

I read this article where doctors say all this emotional heaviness is causing more physical illnesses, like chest pain, the sensation of someone choking you, or nausea. Yes, anxiety is genuine, and the enemy will do whatever he can to keep you there. Do you ever wonder why you are a little anxious after watching the news? The endless amount of paranoia and fear will do that. So let's turn our thoughts to the eternal thinking of heaven.

Promising Moments toward a New Beginning

So many resources have helped me along this highway toward healing. When I realize I'll never see my missing loved one again on this side of eternity, in those "Why, God, Why" moments, my number one calming force is knowing my life here on earth isn't my final destination. Taking our last breath on earth is the beginning of our new life with God. We will have the life we received when we said "Yes" to Jesus and accepted the belief in our heavenly Father and heaven. Our eternal life is the real life God designed and destined for us.

Here's a question for you, friend: When's the last time you stepped outside on a warm summer night, found a quiet and comfortable place, slowed your mind down, leaned back, and looked into the stars? Some of the brightest stars I've ever witnessed were in Yosemite, California, on top of mountains, in the quiet stillness, away from cars and the rush of city life. Relaxing and listening, you might hear nature… an owl hooting or crickets chirping. I love the stars with their many shapes and clusters, like the "big dipper" asterism, and endless stars to count, all spreading their light and beauty throughout the night sky. Even in the lowest valley, there will be the crack of bright moments like light speckled and scattered over the darkest night. The process will be messy but beautiful. Spectators will stand in awe of the beauty they found when everything all seemed so dark.

I want you to give yourself this gift. You could even have a particular quiet spot picked out, so when a night of favorable weather comes along, you will know where to go to check out the heavenly beauty. Open… and clear… your mind and heart. Relax. Slow your breathing and reminisce about all the light and glistening moments in the here and now. Imagine what the view may look like to your loved one.

Remember, no matter how dark your season may look or how lost you may feel, God reminds us heaven is real through many of

His creations, like the stars. One fable says the stars are where the angels poked holes in the sky, so we see the lights from heaven. I like that. The idea brings peace and assurance.

We know our missing person may be gone from our reality here, but that person who went to be with God is there waiting for us. Depression doesn't get the final say. In like manner, we can know broken relationships are also NOT our identity. We can know that like the beauty of diamond stars in the night sky, even in the darkest moments, our God can bring the light of His beauty to all who believe.

Chapter 10

EVERYONE ... EXCEPT ME

I f you are like me, you jump into your bed for an hour of social media after a long day of work. Do you ever notice that even spending thirty minutes on social media may make you think everyone else in the world has everything going for them? You may sense this wave of urgency. All your single friends want to rush onto a dating app, find a man, rush through the "getting-to-know-you" stage, get married, have kids, and throw the most epic gender reveal party ever. I mean, come on, let's be real. How many women do you know set up a Pinterest board for their future wedding ... with the *one* thing missing, the man? Or everyone seems to go on five-star trip when the last time you did anything close to a vacation was a forty-minute drive to your favorite upscale cosmetics store?

No wonder so many people end up disconnected from one another! Even while sitting face-to-face, having a full-on conversation, our minds can be in the past or the future. We are never here and grounded in the moment because in this hi-tech fast-paced instant day and age we are not okay with how slow things are panning out.

Will Anyone Ever Love Me?

We try to do the "Let Go and let God" thing. Live Love Laugh (millennials will get it). Meanwhile, we are trying to control every aspect of our lives. How can we let Jesus be the driver if we have one foot on the brake and the other on the gas?!

I'm never getting married. Why can't I ever be successful? I hate my life. I have no friends. I hate my body. I hear these types of lies from girls often. This type of talk can make somebody put an "I'm Never Going to Make It" sign on their front porch. One big lie I believe many women struggle with is no one will love them, and no one ever loved you in the past, so what makes anything different now. God wouldn't love you. God couldn't repair your broken heart. He couldn't take away the emptiness you feel. All this bad happening all at once, so, of course, no one loves me.

Like most of you, I believed the lie one time or another. I believed God gave everyone else a special favor, and I was this outcast. Not being able to keep up with society's timeline can put you "on edge," overwhelming your body or where you don't want to do anything. Sometimes you can want so much to have what everyone else seems to have and find yourself willing to settle for whatever attention you can get. How can we, as daughters of Christ, love others well if we can't even see how much God loves us?

Betrayal, brokenness, and a big splash of loneliness get you into the arena where the enemy thinks he controls you. When your guards are down, you're in this "I don't care" bubble and whatever comes into your mind is whatever goes. Nothing phases you any longer.

But Jesus … Jesus is your fighting warrior who will help you accept your true worth and dignity. God designed you to accept and live in that kind of life.

When we, as women, go through a breakup or major devastation, we can sometimes be at our very lowest for months afterward.

Our minds aren't aligned. We're extra emotional and lack confidence, and if we are being honest, we aren't functioning up to our known abilities.

We Accept the Unacceptable

You have the need to control life. God's taking forever, so you must step in and do the work. You hurry life up because our biological clock is ticking, and who cares if he isn't a Christian? I mean, "I'm sure I can change him, right?" I mean, "Yeah, sure, he doesn't want to go to church with me?" … but that's okay, right? "Sundays are for the boys," like they say, right? Or you may get pressure from people, "it's been five years of their passing, time to move on." Suppressing your emotions, *I'm not sad*. When asked how you are, you're quick to respond, *I'm fine*. You go through these doubts and fears all while never seeking the professional help you know you need. You may have frozen your gym membership for months when you know you must be there for your mental state.

I want to encourage you, new bestie, if you never heard anyone say to you, "God did not forget you," then I want you to know He sees and loves you beyond what we can comprehend. He hears your heart's desires and knows the pain that has no words.

The challenge of not obsessing over your future—the mindset that could become sticky—leaves you feeling left behind. Trust in God's timing. Celebrate the love stories and restored hearts God brought to others. Be patient with kindness and compassion to and for yourself. Consider God is still writing our life story as long as we have a pulse.

God isn't finished with you yet, sister. Rest today in peace, trusting God to bring you to what He knows is best for you. Trust and believe in Him.

Chapter 11

THANK GOD FOR UNANSWERED PRAYERS

I want to address another serious form of brokenness—heartaches from a breakup. At some point, many of us have suffered through either a breakup, broken relationship, abuse, or infidelity. I wasn't sure what to call this chapter since a relationship has so many aspects of heartache.

I dedicated this chapter title to a season where I prayed the same prayer repeatedly for years over specific relationships. And thank God, He didn't answer those prayers the way I asked. When you are in a relationship you want to work so badly, your prayers can gravitate toward getting what you want and believe is best. You think that if only God were to answer your prayers, then your boyfriend would be the best you can ever get. Sista, I promise you, God's best for you goes beyond and exceeds what you can imagine.

Who Has Your Plate?

I remember attending a girls' night small group when I was a young girl. The lady running the event said something to me I never understood then, but I do now. She was a sweet, single, older lady who had never gotten married because of a breakup she never got over. She brought out a plate and told us when the time comes for us to fall in love; we place our heart on a tray like this and give that plate to someone else. At any point, this plate can drop and shatter and you will try to fix the broken pieces, but you will take years and at some point, the plate will never be the same.

I was about eight years old, and truly did not understand what she meant about heartbreak. Up to that point, the only heartbreaking thing I had experienced was never getting a Pokémon card in the exact version I wanted.

When my dad took his first breath in heaven, I was ready to write and talk about what I was going through, since the trek of his paralysis was part of my whole life's story.

Hi, you guys, my dad's in the wheelchair… something I would say my whole life confidently to new friends. He was my superhero, so why wouldn't I share that? My dad's health was something I was used to talking about. Writing allowed me to grieve and process my pain. However, breakups come with a different set of emotions. People call this a heartbreak for a reason. The sensation is as if your heart is broken in half like that plate—your dreams, the attachments, and memories of all the years being broken into half.

Vulnerable, Not Hopeless

I wasn't ready to express fully my deepest vulnerabilities about the heartaches from broken relationships that scared me deeply. I wanted to keep my brokenness to myself, erase my pain, and move forward.

The enemy wants you to hate, disrespect, and be revengeful with bitterness toward the ones who intentionally, and even those who unintentionally, hurt you. But that's not the way to go. The cheating, breakups, hurts, and all the in-between desperate moments were a lesson or blessing, but for me, they proved to be a lesson I learned more times than I would have wanted.

I do not mean to disrespect men in any way. They, too, are God's children. Yes, what those men in your life did may have been wrong, but holding on to hate and unforgiveness ends up hurting yourself all over again. You can forgive for yourself and still hurt because of what the breakup did to you.

I was in too many broken relationships throughout high school and college and all the way to adulthood. Toxic, broken, and traumatic relationships were all I knew. I've been cheated on, abused, manipulated, and used all while not knowing my worth.

Reflecting, I see the root issue speaking for myself. Going through so much with my dad's situation brought me to where the only thing I truly desired was a man there for me. I didn't recognize Jesus was the only person who can fully restore my heart. Friend, sometimes we try to put up with someone we know deep down inside doesn't deserve a second in our lives. You know you have to walk away, but there's a spark of a promise that the person will be different. May I kindly ask you to take the time to pray about the relationship? I've learned Jesus is not a spirit of confusion and chaos. If you're with someone who brings up those feelings, more than likely, Jesus does not want that relationship to work out. Take the time to reconsider your relationship. You can get all the advice in the world, but in the end, the one who gets to decide what you do is you.

You pray God will bring you through, speak to you, and show you signs. If you really look, you can see the answers you prayed for everywhere you go, like when someone tells a story and speaks one line right to you, and you feel it in your core. I believe what stops us from doing what we know is right is what we all have met more often than we may even think: FEAR.

Fear of Being Alone

No, I'm not talking about a fear of scary things. I am talking about fears deep within us, like fear of being alone on New Year's Eve, of hearing society screaming, you must be married with two kids by a certain age, or fear of betrayal. We can also have a fear of losing our identity, of supposed security, change, or simple trust. And all those can enhance a fear of shame that we have failed God, our families, and ourselves.

This "fear list" could go on and on and on. We need to realize we have control over how we handle fear. We also have the power by God to speak the fear away.

We will all have fear at one point, but here is the truth: GOD does not give us a spirit of fear. Neither does He give us a spirit of anxiety. Our enemy is using these weapons to keep us from God. Of course, not all fear is detrimental. I mean, I fear when I go deep into the ocean I could be that small percentage to run into a great white shark. I like to call these healthy fear human instincts.

If you are in a situation draining your spirit, God could be encouraging you to walk away from the situation or allow Him to work on the change in that relationship. Only you and God know the answer to that.

Anxiety and worries will for sure come up in relationships. The anxiety and worry are telling you it's time to make changes. Maybe you are idolizing your partner over God or failing to keep God first. It might be you're having sex before marriage, knowing this is wrong in God's plan. You might not even remember the last time you went to church. Maybe you're becoming envious of other relationships. God blesses us with good things, but sometimes, good things end when we forget Who provided them to us in the first place.

For myself, in the past the anxiety and worries have come up in many relationships. But looking back, I realize they were red flags waving in my sky, alerting me something was "off," like a big DANGER sign. Sure enough, something was off. God was not trying to work a change in that relationship. God was guiding me with that "stomach drop" moment that something was not part of His plan and I needed to have a heart change.

An ex smashing your head on the car dashboard is not part of God's plan. A man wanting you to drive through a storm at one in the morning to "Netflix and chill" was his selfish desires and not God's plan. A guy breaking up with me on the holidays so that he could spend time with another girl, only to get back with me later: yeah, that wasn't what God wanted for me. A man spitting in my face…also most definitely not ideal. A boyfriend smashing my cell phone and car keys so I couldn't drive was not God's best for me. Okay, maybe I went a little too far with the experiences, and you're thinking… oh, wow, Hannah, why would you even have been okay with that? Because the idea of having *anybody* consumed my mind. Obsessed with having someone is not a good place to be when going through dark seasons.

Moving on Is Okay

Wow, even typing these old memories makes me nauseated to know how much I allowed to be "okay." When you're *in* that relationship, "love can become blind." You question your sanity and how much more you will accept. You start to believe and bury the abuse that maybe you are the problem. IF only you were prettier, maybe he wouldn't have cheated. IF only I wasn't so clingy. IF only lists detouring you to the reality—God did not design this relationship, you are in for you.

Many moments I reached the point of enough. I was done trying to cover the bruises on my leg. I no longer tolerated getting random messages from girls saying they saw him with another girl. I had enough of sitting in the ICU hospital waiting room while being on the phone hearing about how my "bf" at the time was cheating on me. I was done downplaying my true self and conforming to the likes of what he was wanting.

In my most vulnerable moments, I only wanted someone whispering *I'm here for you*. The enemy's prime territory is when you are navigating a breakup, a toxic relationship, or attempting to increase your confidence to leave because you are alone and lonely. He will remind you of all your faults and fears of not being okay without that certain person. You may even hear lies that sound like *you'll never find anyone else. You can't be alone. What if you're single forever? Just put up with the abuse.* I also understand the memories, good times, and moments couples shared are hard to let go.

I learned you don't need to let the memories go. It is okay to look back and see some of those times were good. They might even have been a blessing at some point. But now that blessing became a lesson. In prayer, you can cherish those memories and still love someone from a distance.

You can want the best for them by allowing them to find Jesus on their own. We can't ever control or be God in a man's life. He must find his identity on his own time. Men have emotions as well; they don't express them as much as women do. But they do, unless they are straight bananas.

I put up with someone doing so many unacceptable things to me because I placed my identity in the hands of a man who didn't know what love was. Remember, abuse—whether verbal, emotional, or even financial—is *never* part of God's plan. We are God's daughters, and we must remember we have a Father who will look out for us, love us, and be who our hearts desire. If you didn't have a father figure who brought the sense of safety and love your younger self so desperately desired, you may have sought relationships through that stem of hurt to fulfill that emptiness.

My sweet dad showed me so much love in his precious ways and reminded me he loved me. During soccer games, my dad would wheel himself out on the field whenever I was injured. He would text me every hour asking if I was "k." In translation he was asking *Am I okay?* Even though I felt his love, something was lacking—the physical safety and protection I never got from having a healthy father brought fear to my life.

I was always so afraid at the house. Not knowing how we would defend ourselves if someone were to break in. I have my journal from when I was eight years old. I read an entry of a dream I recorded about me laying in my room with my dad and mom in the other room. I said a robber broke in, and I was so scared for my family, but I know my dad loves me. My younger self was trying to process I knew my dad physically couldn't protect me, but I also knew he deeply loved me. So, through that, I always desired a man to bring that physical security I needed.

When you deal with distress, you encounter a vast open vulnerability you never experienced. Your walls come down and your standards drop. You sometimes even settle for something far less than you deserve.

After my dad passed, I returned to people who didn't respect or value me. I wanted to feel hurt from another person, not the reality of what was happening—the real hurt from someone passing. I didn't care how someone treated me as long as I felt something—anything besides the reality of the truth. Sorrow can cause numbness to come over you like a wave, sometimes creating actions you wouldn't have done. I wasn't thinking straight… well, I wasn't thinking at all. I was in the denial stage when I accepted all the abuse back in again.

My thinking was as if my body was saying, okay, Hannah, your dad didn't die… but you know he did, but you can't think about his passing… so go be with the person who caused the most heartache. Or go back to what you think will be the one who knows you best, but also look past the infidelity.

When we go through severe heartache or allow certain situations to happen that devalue us, the biggest emotion is an abundant showering of shame upon us. Shame screams, you're not worth anything. Wow, look what you did. But I'm here to tell you, kick all those thoughts out the window where they belong—buried in the dirt. No matter how big a mistake you made, God can and will use those mistakes.

Work on being aware of your strengths, weakness, and insecurities and find the roots of why certain things trigger you. Continue doing the steps of triggers as we learned earlier in the book, steps necessary for processing. What are you struggling with deep inside? What habits do you do? What did you alter because of those ruined relationships? Because the real you, the royal precious you, can become and step into who God designed you to be if you surrender your ways and heartaches.

Always trust God is the same yesterday, today, and tomorrow. That same God, who owns and made the whole universe, lives inside you. We have the Holy Spirit's power to breathe life into our shattered shame. Once we establish self-awareness and know God's Holy Spirit is helping us, we will start changing our relationships and get the courage and strength to walk away and say enough is enough. You are the daughter of a king who loves you. Hurt people hurt people, and girlfriend, you are done being hurt by someone who doesn't know even how to love himself.

God Is Your Strength

Once you recognize God is always with you, for you, and fighting frontline battles, why wouldn't He bless your relationships. That is when you can let God change those broken relationships or situations to do what God meant relationships to do: glorify Him. Or that can also mean the clarity of knowing a particular season ended.

When my now husband came back into my life in 2018, I said

a desperate call-for-help prayer just a few weeks before meeting him again. One evening after my birthday dinner, while lying in bed, feeling extra low, hopeless, and lost, I cried out to God for Him to remove anyone and anything that was not part of His plan. I wanted a new fresh year. And believe me, I've prayed that plenty of times in the past, but after my dad passed and I went back to old unhealthy relationships, I was in a place of complete surrender.

After praying with a hurting heart, I got a text a few days later. God brought back a man, who so happened to be my first kiss when I was just fourteen and the rest truly is history. My best friend (aka husband) is the total exact opposite of what I envisioned my future husband to be, but I can say wholeheartedly, he is exactly what I needed. Friend, give Jesus the pen to write your love story. He will not give what you want, but what you need.

Focus on your relationship with God. Step back and allow Jesus to be God in your partner's life. You can never change another person. You can only change yourself. If that relationship ends, who knows? Perhaps you were the closest thing to Jesus that person ever had. Maybe through your forgiveness, he will see Jesus.

Focus on doing you with Jesus in the center of your life.

You don't need to look for an answer, sign, or clarification. Seeking those things can block what God wants us to do—TRUST HIM. But if you are looking for a sign, HERE IS YOUR SIGN.

Seek Him. Love others.

Dive into His Word today, sister. Journal your internal struggles and the actions to certain behaviors you know you have. Pray for your partner. This is a spiritual battle God can help you fight. You are not bonkers, but being with the wrong one can bring chaos and disturbance from the enemy.

Your broken heart is ready to beat again.

Now, put that waterproof mascara back on, go make yourself some cold brew, and slay away the day, you wonder warrior.

Chapter 12

A SACRIFICE ON EARTH VERSUS A GAIN IN HEAVEN

The other day, I was chatting with my "twin," a.k.a. "mom," when something she said hit home. She said she became immune to loss. And the truth is she was right. I feel like I have, too. Since the major loss of my dad, I've heard the line, "he passed away," or "she didn't make it" more times than ever before. Maybe our age seems to swing on by, but to feel immune to death is different. Before I would hear of a death rarely, and now I seem to hear of them each month.

I'm learning I used to fear death, never wanting to talk about my life ending on earth. My friend, we will ALL take our final breath on this side of eternity. No one lives forever. Others told me I was wrong for fearing death, but I believe when we go through such a tragic loss, fearing another death from a loved one or yourself is something we can't help.

Beauty beyond What We Can Imagine

The Bible gives us beautiful glimpses of heaven: streets made of gold, the singing, no more pain, and the sweet reunions with our people. But we don't know what will happen until we get there.

I've heard multiple stories of people encountering death, coming back to life, and explaining what they went through. While those stories can become super controversial, to me in a way they bring a sense of curiosity. I enjoy being curious because I learn. Being curious and learning is a form of healthy healing.

I never remember my dreams, unless I awaken myself, feeling as if I'm about to fall out of a tree. I recalled a particular dream a few weeks before releasing my debut book.

I dreamed of this beautiful, vivid encounter with Jesus. The setting was in a very large landscape, still and serene. I saw two birds flying over green mountains. In front of me, I saw a man with long, brown hair. I didn't see his legs, but he wore a pure white outfit, which seemed like a robe. With His head down, he slowly appeared before me, as he looked up. He smiled with eyes bright and blue like the ocean, and so much electricity and power coming from them. Even though He smiled saying nothing, He approached me. I felt He shared so much through that brief moment. Jesus somehow allowed me to enjoy His presence in creation as I saw birds fly throughout the sky. He then appears and comes to me—pursuing me like He always did. With no words, He shows the power in what is silence, but in reality, the words of His strength. That, my friend, is the same strength we can have in our heart through the Holy Spirit.

I believe one of the biggest fears in losing our person is the separation of not being with them forever. The connection and attachment to that person and separating from them is one pain no one can describe.

What brought me peace on earth while mourning is the truth. If we both have accepted Jesus into our lives, we are hanging out on this earth for a few decades until we enter paradise together. That's why we must spend quality time with our person, making sure they know their destiny, and you know yours as well. Heaven is our real home, and the earth we are living in is a fancy hotel.

Changing Our Focus

As much as becoming immune to death sounds off, giving those thoughts our attention is strange and weird. Once we become immune to loss, our perspectives change while still on earth. We have an eternal perspective. Our stresses, priorities, and actions change because we know we will head to heaven. Our goals slowly align in another direction. That next trend the world keeps marketing you to buy no longer seems as significant.

Does our changed thinking remove the sting? No! Does our eternal perspective not make death eerie? No. At times, I still cannot grasp the concept of death, like here one day, gone the next. This concept won't come into my mind as something I get about the truth of heaven being forever, like forever ever? No time? I'll never get that mind wrap. But thinking about heaven gives us the extra hype to get us back on track, knowing we will see our favorite person again.

I talk to my dad daily, more so when I can't handle his absence. I tell him what I'm expecting of him and what I want to do when I get to heaven. One day, I asked my dad if he would make us Korean barbeque in heaven. I want to enjoy a barbeque at sunset on the beach, and we will dig our feet deep into the warm sand. Then, Jesus, me, and my baby Chihuahua Mocha and Chanel could be the taste testers. Yup, that's how specific I can be.

I encourage you to try that. Write out and speak out what you're hoping to do and see in heaven. Get creative. Let your imagination run wild. What kind of house you want. Who do you want to be your neighbors? Let your mind get crazy. I envision God smiling when He hears our sweet, dreamy imaginations.

Someone once told me God will assign us jobs in heaven. You will do what you truly love doing. My dad chose to be a doctor, so I would like to imagine him running his own clinics and hospitals in heaven in his own special way. I know there won't be sick people in heaven. But I would like to allow my imagination to flow and picture him flying helicopters and airplanes in heaven throughout his doctor's office.

I would encourage you to imagine what your loved one may be doing in heaven. Did they love golf? Maybe he is playing some epic golf tournaments. Did she love to draw? Maybe she's in charge of drawing up the painting for heaven in the sky that we on earth can see. Did he love to drink coffee? Perhaps he oversees running a coffee shop in heaven, and when you sip your favorite drink, you can almost sense their love.

My friend, the sky is the limit about what they could be doing now. I can assure you; they truly are living their best lives.

You see, friend, until that magical day, we still have a God who never leaves us. On earth, we have God right next to us and His Holy Spirit in us. When we breathe our first breath in heaven, God will be right there with us forever.

So, let us not fear death. Let us anticipate our future and brainstorm ideas for what heaven will be. God's final home for us will be far better than we could ever dream of or imagine. Every day is a day closer to your real home.

Chapter 13

WALKING THE AISLE
WITHOUT YOU

Learning how to soak in the joy and sorrow that comes when planning, attending, and being in a wedding when our loved one is not here can be a challenge.

Okay, so you got engaged, and you're in the middle of the wedding plans for your Big Day. Congratulations! But without warning, a rush of emptiness and gloom overwhelms you. You notice the now familiar, but unwanted, aching flowing back over, around, and into every crevice of your soul. You are reliving the reality your lost loved one won't be there to walk you down the aisle or see you say, "I do." They won't be there for the first dance or to laugh or cry happy tears with you.

Someone very close to me recently married. I felt that same emptiness, choking me when I realized I could not share the closeness of sitting next to my lost one, witnessing such a beautiful marriage. That lost part of my soul was not there to share a text with or call about the wedding.

When I thought about my wedding planning and attending another wedding, I realized this was a new milestone in my trauma.

I now had yet another new adjustment of how to navigate what I was going through. Guilt creeps in for being sad; you feel lost and that you don't deserve this, or you even feel selfish. Whether you're a soon-to-be bride, already a bride, a family member of someone getting married, or a wedding guest, I want to help you with this new mission, speak life, and encourage you. Everything you are feeling in this new season is okay. You're okay. You have pain because you love. Just because a few years passed or however long since you lost your loved one doesn't mean the road is easy.

Your Lost Loved One Would Want Your Wedding to Be Special

I lost my dad in my prime years when many of my friends were getting married. My future wedding was something my dad and I joked and talked about. At my dad's nursing home where he lived his last six years, we would often sit in his room, with alarms going off in every corner and laugh about what that special day would look like. We joked about how we would walk down the aisle and how my dress might get stuck in his wheels or I may sit on his lap as he wheeled himself. After chatting, he would electric wheel himself into the lobby. I'd open the door for him before I exited, and he watched me drive away back home to then me honking loud stating my love for him. I would see his contented smile, knowing I was safe.

Driving away now feels like the countless memories of our wedding plans burned in the air on the day my dad took his last breath.

A few months after my dad passed, I was part of a wedding where I watched one of my friends walk down the aisle with her dad. I stood right in the front. I couldn't talk to anyone because, first, this wasn't my day. And who in their right mind would ask for comfort and spoil the happy mood of a good friend's wedding? I sat in front at the reception, watching the father-daughter dance. I knew at any moment I was about to burst into tears. Month after month, I attended additional weddings, and the same emptiness was there.

I was engaged in 2020. What a bittersweet time. I was so happy, but not having my dad there was always in the forefront of my thoughts. I'm learning sorrow and joy can be present in me at the same time, whether at weddings, graduation, or whatever occasion. Any big special event comes with joy and sorrow. We are here to learn to navigate and be okay through both emotions, joy and sorrow.

Navigating the Grief and Sorrow in the Joyful Moments

Once I became engaged and started planning my wedding, the biggest challenge was the heavy sorrow of not having my dad. And there was very little community understanding of my pain. None of my friends lost a parent. Therefore, I never heard, "I get how you're feeling." I was so alone. I felt as if no one understood what I was going through. But 100 percent of the time I heard, "I can't even imagine if I lost a parent." Well, I don't want to speak for anyone else, but I can sure attest to the majority. I don't think any of us could have ever imagined… but were we given a choice!?

Even though the grief community seems small, I know because of our world's size, others have lost a loved one before their "big day." Maybe you watched a brother or sister walk down the aisle alone. You might have been a wedding guest, feeling that sting when you saw the father escorting the bride to the front. Or maybe you're the maid of honor and watched in sadness and envy as your best friend danced with her father. You feel horrible for these thoughts because this is the happiest moment of their lives, yet you're drowning, fighting back the tears.

So, my question to you, my dear friend, is: How can one be okay in moments like these? How can you say, "I do" without having the one you loved sitting there in the front row? How can you watch your best friend make her way along the aisle on her father's arm? How can you celebrate those big moments while you are grieving? How can you honor your loved one without them being there?

The pages you are reading are a safe place for you to "feel" … a time for you to grieve … a time for you to laugh … a time for you to hope again. This is a time for you to "love forward" with your person in your heart.

I designed this book to be a simple read on purpose. Let's be real—moving forward after a parting is a lifelong season to endure, and being a maid of honor, bridesmaid, or the bride is a legit job. As I'm writing this book, I still have three-day-old curls from my cousin's wedding, which reminds me I should probably lay off the dry shampoo and shower.

Days before a very important individual of my life got married; I planned my maid of honor speech. As in the previous years, I felt an overwhelming emptiness, sadness, and, to be honest, anger. The previous lies I played in my head came creeping back in. "okay, Hannah, stop, this is not your day… focus… show no tears… don't think about what is making you sad."

But I couldn't help the emotions erupting within. I almost thought God was playing favoritism. I thought about the despair creeping in and how unfair life seems for the other daughters out there who will never have a dad to walk them to the altar. How do some girls have that first dance with their dads while others have no one? But then those thoughts become this mental fight in your mind where you try not to reflect on the situation because you don't want to be selfish in thinking of yourself. You have a constant fight in your mind while smiling at the other guests. So, you stuff your feelings down later to burst into tears when someone asks how you are. Volcano grief is what I'd call these unpredictable moments.

I was talking to a gal the other day who lost her mom. She mentioned how angry and upset she feels because her mom won't be there on the big day to watch her sister marry her dream boy. She said her mom passed away months before the boy came into her sister's life. My response was simply to just listen. I don't know why God allows some people to have a dad, and others to lose a dad. Why some will have a father-daughter dance, and how some will not. I know I have some unanswered prayers on this side of eternity I'll need to deal with until I reach heaven when God will give me all the answers.

Wedding Gloom Is Real

I googled books about "grieving a loss before a wedding." I found nothing. I reworded my search ... "how to handle a wedding during a loss." There was still nothing. Then, "how to prepare for a wedding as a guest after loss of a loved one" ... Nada. Of course, many books are available on how to grieve under the topic "loss." My debut book, *Never Goodbye*, discusses a lot about that. Now, I am talking about how to handle nuptial ceremonies ... getting married ... being a guest at a wedding ... being in a wedding. All that got me started thinking.

The wedding industry is huge. Each year, countless couples marry. That's many weddings, emotions, stress, and happy tears. Let's also consider those who now have to face not having those special moments with their beloved parent who passed on.

If I'm struggling here four years after my dad's passing as a soon-to-be bride, there must be others out there with these same heart-wrenching emotions. If my stomach is still turning while attending weddings, watching father-daughter dances, dads walking their daughters down the aisle, or even seeing a memory table, I know others have these same bittersweet emotions.

I included a part in this book for those going through the wedding adventure. Planning a wedding alone is emotional enough, but when you plan your big day without the parent you lost, you endure the next level of hurt.

When talking to the different vendors in the beginning, I explained to each one there would be no father-daughter moment. Having to repeat the same statement aloud almost created this self-pity elephant in the room. Saying the words aloud caused my father's absence to become more real. As excited as I was planning my wedding with my mom, we both agreed the sadness of not having my dad there was heartbreaking.

I sometimes even imagined how my wedding would be different if my dad were around. I would envision my dad and me planning my wedding with my dad being present, later realizing how much time I wasted on that. Looking back, I realized I didn't waste the time. I was grieving what could've been and learning to accept that. You're living a new normal, friends, be understanding, flexible, and gentle with what your mind processes.

Love Balloons to Heaven

Well, it happened! The days, tears, planning, and laughing all leading up to our special day on September 18, 2022, at Saddleback Church in San Juan Capistrano (also referred to as "The Ranch") is the day my husband became the luckiest man by saying I do to me. Ha ha, jokes aside, we said I do.

I've always wanted to get married on a church and having a rustic ranch with a splash of glamour. Well, God couldn't have been better than providing this perfect ground—a beautiful, 170-acre oasis nestled in the foothills of South Orange County. An air of peace and serenity filled the grounds, making anywhere at our venue an ideal location to relax, heal, and experience God's love everywhere we went.

I could probably write a whole other book going into detail about this beautiful day. But to keep it simple, we had a truly beautiful wedding and more, with a few tears here and there. It was a vow and sacred moment in front of all our family and friends becoming one. In the days leading up to this marriage, I journaled my heart out in prayer and words about how to prepare my heart for the day I talked about with my dad when I was a little girl.

I knew I wanted to make sure all my family was part of the ceremony. I had my mom and brother walk me down the aisle, and before we walked down, I said a prayer to my dad and looked to the skies. I made sure to have my whole family part of this day. My *halmoni* (Korean grandma), all my aunts, uncles, cousins, and niece and nephew were part of the wedding and representing our Korean culture by wearing *hanboks*, a traditional Korean dress.

I knew my dad was there with us. I felt his love and presence everywhere from the love we received by everyone around us. I wanted to make sure I honored my dad, and kept him part of this day in a special way. We honored his life by doing a balloon release with his favorite colors. As my good friend Amy beautifully played his favorite song on the violin, others in the crowd who had lost someone released a balloon.

My mom walked around the tables and gave a balloon to one individual at each table. This was my way of honoring my dad and the others who also had lost someone. As we released the balloons, we were in a way sending our love to heaven, remembering and reflecting on life. After the wedding, I felt so much love, hurt, and joy all at the same time. I was missing my dad and over-stimulated by everything that just happened and at the same time, I felt so much love.

Did I miss my dad at the wedding? Yes, but did I create new lifelong memories with family and friends and enter into a new season of life as a wife? Yes, I knew my dad was cheering me on and saw all the pain, anxiety, and hurt leading up to our wedding. But I also knew my dad would want me to smile and laugh and enjoy every moment.

Friends, God promises to bring newness to all the years and months that have been our story. I never thought I'd marry, but you see, God knew. He knew all along that day, I'd stand with all the pain at that altar as he created the new Hannah that afternoon. The season of newness is upon each of you.

I designed different chapters for the different seasons you may be in. You may not have reached those "seasons" yet, but you know you will one day. You can go back to any chapter in this book for your comfort and encouragement anytime.

My prayer, sister, as you continue your pathway in this life, is to please, please be gentle and compassionate with yourself, no matter how much time has passed. Don't hold back the tears. Experience the emotions. The days of survival mode of fright or flight with white knuckles are ending today.

Chapter 14

FOCUS MODE

PING, PING, PING, PING. Twenty-six notifications later, you wake to unread emails and text messages from days ago—deadlines to make. Maybe you're planning a wedding or some other monumental event coming up, and you want to reach a certain goal.

Distractions are everywhere from scrolling with your thumb. I think that's why the iPhone designed the "focus" tab, which mutes the noise.

Scroll Less

I mean, talk about overstimulating the mind! All social media avenues contribute to keeping your mind in a constant uproar. The silence in the room may sound louder than your preoccupied thoughts.

I'm a social media butterfly. I love the way you can express yourself through the various platforms. I know you may need to market and promote your business to grow. Trust me, I understand, girl! As an author, social media marketing is part of my routine each day. I love helping other people's businesses in different industries, so I often get cool gifts where I am required to post and share my opinion. People call this "a social influencer." I prefer to call myself "a friend" because that's what friends do: promote and help others.

This chapter isn't about me telling you to delete all your apps. But I am suggesting the possibility that when you're having your "grief" moments, sit with them rather than scroll through other lives. Tune into what your body is doing when you are going through an episode to honor your body and make progress in recovering by taking the breaks you need.

Are there days I spend a little more time on social media than usual? Absolutely. Are there moments when I also deactivate all mine to give my mind a break for a week? Yes. I am trying to encourage you to be true to your heart, and balance needs to be the key. With a ton of information coming into our minds, sometimes it's hard to do that. Friend, when we intentionally occupy our minds over feeling our true grief with creating our next video, hashtag, or insta-worthy photos, we continue to unintentionally push down our buried hurts and painful emotions even further without even recognizing what we are doing. Then, we may start caring more about our online followers than our true friends who want to be there for us. Living in the twentieth century, I am almost certain you've seen photos of people "hanging out," but what you see was not the reality. Some of you may have even been there in person to see everyone hanging out to be on their phone.

A longtime friend and I went out to dinner, and I had to photograph every moment of that evening. I photographed me eating, me talking to the waiter, and her eating. Believe me when I tell you, I love taking photos, but let's pause for some time to enjoy the moment...I may be preaching to myself.

Distractions Won't Help You Process

I realized the importance of appreciating the stillness a few days ago, and I paused to take in the present. Often, I get so "into" the spiral of the noise and distractions that, even if I stop for a moment, a heavy sadness comes rushing in. Does anyone else out there wake up feeling sad? Or does it seem like nothing is going right for you? You may remember answered prayers, but you might be a little blurry-eyed because of a lack of mental focus?

I walked into a bookstore. On a front bookstand, I saw *Never Goodbye* displayed next to some cool Christian authors I adore. As I stood there, I realized I was feeling … nothing. This was the same bookstore my dad and I used to frequent. A few years after he passed, I stood there and prayed God would give me the wisdom to write that book sitting there on the bookstand facing me. Here I was … numb. Sometimes I wonder: Am I going crazy? No. I realized what I saw was not registering in my mind with the other twenty thousand things in the queue. My mind was saying "Uh … Hello? Let me catch you up so that you can process all this."

Process is a word telling us to break down, work through our emotions, and become aware of our physical state. What was I doing a lot these past days? Hmm… Oh, let me check my screen time. YUP … way too much screen time.

A few days back, I took a break to lie down and close my eyes to rest. Why did I bawl? My once-a-month woman moment was not even close, so the crying couldn't be my hormone-related emotions. No, the hurt and misery still sitting there—unresolved, untouched, and not even acknowledged—overcame me. My soul was giving me a reminder. "Umm … Hey, we have some soul work to do here." I believe dealing with our brokenness is God's way to get us back on track, align us, and bring us back "beside the still waters" that lead us to still calmness and peace.

Working through heartaches takes time—a lot of time. Not just months or even years. I believe the process will become a lifelong task because of habits you formed, such as from a toxic relationship that created an identity in you. Losing a loved one may have triggered an intense sadness in you because of an upcoming event. You realize you keep wishing they could be there with you. For me, the wedding planning kept reminding me my dad was not here. So many emotions! But I love how God says when we are weak, He is strong. And though it may be a life long journey of healing, it then becomes character and that's what we take into eternity.

God Is Stronger than Our Pain

Yes, we will have our weak moments. Our invitation leaves room for God's strength to create in us a resilient power no man can shut down. In Him, you are a strong woman. We can be incredible superheroes because we have the Holy Spirit within us. We have many wonderful attributes instilled in us from birth, and we must use and see them "grow" every time we use them. This God is the same One who split the Red Sea, caused the blind to see, and loves you more than anyone else could. God wants you to work through all those hurts.

Jesus wants you to put aside the world's distractions for a moment and acknowledge the season you are in. Feel and see the prayers and blessings you're experiencing. Allow the brokenness when you're in those rough patches.

The thorn in my heartache helps me learn to keep my mind on the eternal heaven and not allow the world's many distractions to numb my mind and keep me from what really matters. If I don't keep my mind in check, the numbness will again create isolation from God. Isolation is the enemy's playground. I must remember to honor my dad by honoring Jesus. And you, too, can continue to honor your loved one by honoring Jesus. Continue to pray for the constant renewal of your mind and rewiring of your thoughts.

Friends, when life is dragging you down, and your thoughts are blurry, listen to God through what your body and emotions are telling you. Consider where the sensations are and place your hand over the area. Acknowledge the presence and pray the trauma, pain, and misery will loosen.

Sometimes that is God's signal to you: "Take life easy." When you "hear" yourself wondering why you are so tired and sense you need more rest, turn your thoughts back to God. Consider what you have been learning that would help you ease your sadness and troubled mind.

Let us continue to align our thoughts and actions to get back to what God called us to do on this earth. And accepting Jesus and having a relationship with Him is on the top of that calling for each of us. For us to fulfill our purposes, we must remove the world's distractions and accept the stillness. The peace and serenity can become our lifestyle if we lay aside the control and remember the blessings back into our lives.

Chapter 15

THE BEAUTY IN
SLOWING DOWN

D o you ever have one of those weeks where every song brings tears to your eyes? And I'm not talking about wedding songs. I'm talking about fast, upbeat music… songs intended to get you up and dancing. I'm also not talking about a week we females must endure "chocolate hunger" or salted food cravings, if you're like me. This is one of those seasons where you are so emotional and, oh, so… tired. This tiredness is not from all those attempted ten thousand steps or your cycling class; this is an emotional draining causing your body to be tired.

You feel you ran a marathon, but the only running you did was in your mind. Or maybe there weren't any running thoughts, but a blank mind. Yup, those words would describe me now, and sometimes for over a week. Months. Or, for the first year after my dad passed, I had one whole year of constant drainage.

Sometimes, everything made me cry—a conversation with a friend, a song, or a work interview that was supposed to be positive and lighthearted. They all left me bawling my eyes out … you know, the "ugly" type of cry. The one that makes your face build these two lines between your eyebrows.

God Is With Us in the Ugly

I found many times were my most intimate moments with God during the season when all I could do was cry. I asked myself why I was so emotional, but my body was catching up with my broken heart. My broken heart was catching up with my mind.

Sometimes those moments get us to soul-search our cry to deal with what we are going through. These are often very "raw" hurts. They will rise to the surface in your present moment-to-moment daily life, often with no warning.

In everything I write, with every page and word, I want to be as real as possible about what I'm going through. I believe restoring our mental and emotional wellbeing begins when we learn to be real and name the problems aloud. This will often pinpoint a pathway back to why we feel the way we do. I'm not suggesting you go around telling everyone your deepest hurts. Maybe what might be helpful is having one or two "sisters in Christ" who you trust not to pass on any of what you share with them. The Word says with two or three together seeking Jesus, He is present. "For where two or three gather in my name, there am I with them" (Matthew 18:20 NIV).

With Jesus there, I know He sees my hurts and struggles.

One day, you, too, can recover from your agony and use your experiences to step alongside another gal going through what you went through. Then, she can go on and do the same and be a part of the cycle of shared healing with God. I like to call it the grief cycle. We can do this together as a community, a sisterhood, and as those who can step alongside each other's stories without judgment and share love.

During the months before my wedding, I was busy with wedding plans and catching up on the flurry of writing and publishing my first book. So many blessings came from that. With book touring and all that amazingness, I built new friendships and made magical moments. Much good came to me. Some would even say, "This is your year, Hannah." God was answering my prayers, yet here I am … crying?

My crying makes little sense. The truth is best and makes sense because I am grieving. You aren't alone if you've had these types of outbursts and cries when everything around you is going so well—more than well.

No, Not So Fast

When we go so fast through life, always hopping into the fast lane as if we drank twenty shots of espresso, sometimes our emotions don't keep up. I don't recall any verse stating, "I declare you go so fast in your life that you end up crying, and anxiety overtakes you." No, I don't think the Bible says those words anywhere.

I learned in this "rush" season, when we do too much, our body waves the white flag of surrender, slowing us down. Maybe your mind is going nonstop, overthinking. That "white flag" may develop into chest heaviness. You may become hypersensitive and get offended easy. Then the white flag may feel like you're an outsider watching your life passing by, like a movie. You may have intrusive thoughts you never even thought of before. You're not yourself. If these hidden hurts and emotions continue to emerge faster and faster, you may even erupt like a volcano.

Our loving God is a Father who wants to bring comfort. In this rush season, that may be hard for you to believe. When I am in a whirlpool of rush, I sometimes I question God out loud why certain people have to suffer, and many do not. Why do many girls get to have their father walk alongside them down the aisle at their weddings, but I don't? Why did some of my "friends" never show up when I needed them the most? Why does life just seem plain unfair? The questions are endless.

Through all this, Jesus was teaching me was the beauty of

slowing down. This was a time to question, cry, smile, and have all those in-between feelings during our season of surrender. We get down to the "nitty-gritty" of our emotions in this stillness of slowing down.

Overcoming with Jesus

We may think we have overcome or mastered some hurts with to-do lists. You may think you conquered your pain but didn't even go through the process. You ran through and went around but didn't go through what you needed to. Who would want to live through the hurts that come with those tough seasons? I know I don't. But I also know it is necessary to heal and move forward. Jesus wants you to learn to lean on Him and let Him help you break down and process all the heartaches and pains.

Jesus will help us bring out the present burdens we carried from the past, and He will lighten the burden as they try to linger in our future. Accepting Jesus means we will always have an enemy trying to steal the joy back and trying everything to bring us back to the New York hustle-and-bustle lifestyle. The enemy will use those heartaches to make you feel bleak.

My friend, I'll never know what you went through, the magnitude of your sorrows, or any details that brought so much agony into your heart. I know Who sees and knows everything, and He can see your deep hurt.

Don't run away from your anguish any longer or dodge your feelings from this point on. Knowing Jesus cares so much, sit with the pain. Grab your journal and find comfort in writing what's going on in your mind.

Beauty doesn't come from perfect lives or mended hearts, either. Beauty comes from the ashes. Jesus specializes in making over the old to become new. Lean into Him as hard as necessary. He knows your need. Cry, scream, and be honest with Jesus. He can handle what you are going through. Allow your heart to absorb God's flow of soothing rain. My sister, you've got this. I'm rooting for you.

Now, light your favorite candle. Sip your tea. Sit back, look at all of creation, and thank God for His glory. This is the simplicity of slowing down, which is this gift we call being in the present.

Chapter 16

NOT THE END–YOU'RE GOING TO BE OKAY

I learned by time and through God's love we can hold multiple grudges, burn bridges, and even not empathize during another person's struggles, but in the end, we're hurting ourselves by stalling our recovery. For the last few years, I can sit here today and thank God for the grace and compassion I have toward others (not by my own power).

The ones who didn't come to the hospital when my dad was sick, check up on me, or attend his celebration of life; I couldn't get myself to forgive. I broke those relationships. Those thoughts of unforgiveness and grudges are no longer sitting in my heart. They may come and peek their head out from time to time, but through some heavy prayers, God has brought a newness in my soul to see people for who they are—people. We built the bridges back together and left the grudges in the past where they belong.

In this chapter, I wanted to touch on how you can be that go-to friend with understanding for those who are hurting. Whether you personally experienced grief or never have, learning to stand alongside the hurting is something we can all continually learn.

Throughout the year, I have had multiple people ask me how they could comfort a friend who lost someone, so I hope this chapter brings you that loving knowledge to provide the words and actions to others.

Some people don't realize that when someone is grieving, no matter what time of the day it is, their sensitivity will be at an all-time high or feel at an all-time low. Nothing in between when it comes to emotions. A simple line someone said can bring a roller-coaster of heightened emotions that'll make them feel as if the world is crumbling down. Understand it's nothing about what you said, but rather what they are dealing with in their journey of grief. Grievers hold onto emotions, so as innocent as the comment may be, learning beforehand what might be helpful is crucial.

I'm going through a lot right now. When I heard someone speak those words to me when I was in the middle of my deep sadness and heartache, the last thing I ever wanted to hear was someone telling me they were going through "a lot right now." You're thinking, um, well, did you have to hold the hands of your passing dad?! It's almost as if when you're going through your despair, the only one who should have sorrow and having a difficult time is you. Since I didn't want to hear or even try to empathize with the words others spoke about their struggles, I dissociated myself from others.

Okay, so I'm not saying don't express yourself to someone grieving, but rather, when speaking, allow yourself to have more sensitivity on the topics. Instead of speaking about what you're going through, why not make the topic about all the new things you'd like to try with your grieving friend. These are small adjustments.

You see, there are simple ways to go about when speaking with a grieving friend. These next sections will provide you possible resources.

You Do Want to Help, but Don't Know How

I learned some people don't know how to comfort someone strug-gling—not because they don't care (or maybe some but we don't have time for those), but most of the time, they don't know how to handle what you're going through. How you would've handled coming alongside someone else is not how someone else would have been there for you. I would always say, *I would have been there for you,* but that doesn't change how that person would have supported me if that makes sense.

Maybe you're that child, teen, or young adult not knowing how to handle when someone is going through difficult situations of hav-ing a loved one facing illness or death. Maybe you just lost a mom, and while you're leaving the hospital, you see your friends laughing, having a good time on social media.

Your first instinct is to get bitter and automatically have this sense in your mind, "um, they shouldn't be happy, they should be here with me walking me to my car, I mean I just lost my mom." Friend, first off, I am terribly sorry you are feeling this. Your pain is valid.

How friends live their life during a painful time in your life has nothing to do with how they care for you. People will continue their lives as they should, but that doesn't mean they don't care about you or your pain.

Presence and Action

I believe when people are dealing with dark seasons, two specific actions can bring the biggest source of compassion to them. Whether they are dealing with chronic health, death, or a paralyzed loved one, they will appreciate *the gift of presence* and *the gift of action.*

Perhaps you can share with them through an open honest loving conversation on how they can support you better during this time. Most people don't know how to help and support someone when they are suffering. To make things more complicated, each person will have different needs, so even if your friends found effective ways to support the last person they knew who suffered, they may need to do things differently to help you with what you need.

And for the friends, who were not aware of how their social media happy lives were affecting their friend, give them the gift of action. Do things differently, and be more sensitive and aware of your actions and turn that around and show the loving action you would have wanted for yourself if that was you going through that loss.

Maybe you have a disabled parent. You look at others and see how their lives seem so fulfilled to have a healthy parent. Friend, I struggled my entire life battling that. But the days I prayed to have the eyes of Jesus and heart of God, I could look at those relationships and laugh along with the joyous times they had.

Or maybe you are going through a chronic illness and don't see the light in the tunnel. You live everyday wondering when the next bad news will come. Friend, God sees you. Your pain, struggles, and never-ending bad reports do not go unseen. It's not fair. What you're going through is not fair. How much of life that has been robbed and now you're feeling for your family for what seems to be now more a burden, that's all not fair. I am sorry this is the story you're living.

My dad would often ask at the nursing home, lying in his bed, looking at the ceiling, "what is life?" Life, friends, is believing before seeing. Hoping by faith, one day and one second at a time that what your illness may have done and is doing does not have the final say. Have the strength to muster through the mud and rise above by God's power that what the enemy will try to use to destroy your mental and physical health, God will use to rebuild you.

Love on your friends who have a disabled parent or spouse even if you have zero experience with handling someone in a wheelchair. No need to feel awkward. You can break the ice by speaking life through a compliment and having a light spirit. They may seem fine on the outside, but internally they may have this ache.

Ask the questions when the time is right and they are open to chatting. Ask with a genuine heart how they are feeling, how they are doing, and how you can be there for them. Get creative on ways to keep her special parent part of fun outings. Be aware of whether that place you're going to is disability friendly (has an elevator, ramp, and table space they can join along). You can call ahead at restaurants if necessary. This is the gift of action.

About a month ago, I attended a good friend's wedding. When I saw her dancing with her dad and walking down that aisle, my heart was genuinely happy. I was happy to see the joy she was having. I laid my life to the side, and realized it wasn't about me; it was about her. That's healing, friends, and that takes time.

Or maybe you're that friend or family member on the outside seeing your person struggle with grief. Perhaps you are sympathizing with a friend who just lost a brother, a sister who just lost a best friend, or a cousin who just lost a dad. You're thinking, "Hannah, how am I supposed to comfort them? I have no idea how losing a loved one feels." Okay, you don't have to say anything. You just show up, and you do that by being there for them. You allow them to grieve and honor their person, but you then reassure your friend you are there for them not just through your words but also by your actions. Here are a few scenarios to give you some ideas about how you can demonstrate presence and action:

- **A single mom lost a husband.** You and some friends can muster time to drop of groceries, fix a broken sprinkler, or tidy up her front yard. See, you're honoring her space and time to grieve, yet revealing you are there for her. This is the gift of presence and action.
- **A girl lost her dad.** You can send her a special handwritten letter in the mail on his birthday, Father's Day, or the first holidays without them. You can text them their dad's

favorite song. You don't need to have the right words to say; your gift action is worth more than you can ever speak.

- **Someone at the nursing home isn't in the best shape.** You bring the gift of presence for however long you can, whether five minutes, five seconds, or five hours. That time you decided to visit shows that person they matter, and you offered the gift of presence. My dad absolutely despised being alone at the nursing home and hospitals, so whenever people came throughout the day to visit, when I say it made his day—it really made his day. Sitting there with them. Pulling up a chair, bringing it next to the bed, watching the television show they are watching or hearing their story if they feel up to talk are all the gift of presence. I had friends who showed up at the nursing home and hung out with my dad on the days I was out of town.

Showing you care when someone is hurting or needs help doesn't have to be complicated. We often forget that sometimes, the little things we can do are huge to someone else. For example, I was very appreciative and felt loved when I experienced these small gestures:

- Friends who brought a devotional book to the hospital for me to read
- Someone dropped off my favorite flowers on the doorstep when I got home
- People brought me my favorite coffee drink in the emergency room
- Those who sat with me as I sat with my dad
- Those who showed up without asking

These, my friends, are what you call showing up by the gift of action. But if someone else doesn't do similar thoughtful things, it doesn't mean they don't care.

Recognizing the Intentions

I'm learning when I hear the words of friends, strangers, or even family members who offer their sympathy, comfort, or condolences with no intention of hurting me still hurt. As hard as I tried not to get offended, I did. Throughout this recovery process, I've realized the person speaking the words doesn't know what they are saying is painful. So, you can go about this in two ways. You can let the other person know you would rather not speak about this topic. You can use kind words to bring awareness that you aren't ready to hear the words yet. Or you can listen and understand the person will never understand the pain, but is trying their best to bring comfort to you in some way. So, the keywords here I would say are learning to be understanding, compassionate, and forgiving (even without an apology). Realize they aren't trying to offend you; they are trying their best to comfort you.

Learning to be okay with and accept how others handle rough times takes a lot of forgiveness and compassion.

Who I was the first year of grief to the Hannah I am today took time. God doesn't have timelines. He's more concerned about your heart over time. You take all the time, boundaries, and self-care you need to rebuild your heart and learn the new normal and new formed relationships bound to change over time. But please, learn from me, the bitterness and resentment toward others will not enhance or bring that healing.

The Bible tells us to, "Be kind to one another, tenderhearted,
forgiving one another, as God in Christ forgave you."
Ephesians 4:32 ESV

But the fruit of the Spirit is love, joy, peace,
patience, kindness, goodness, faithfulness.
Galatians 5:22 ESV

I write these pages from my heart … my personal heart moments. I believe the community we develop with others is one of the keys to our emotional wellbeing. God designed us for relationships. We can't progress on our own. You may not always think you are moving forward, but when you notice even a little progress, celebrate the moment. Treat yourself to that burger at In-N-Out (with extra special sauce).

The encouragement from community helped me with the idea every day, every minute, and every second is bringing us that much closer to the time we will again spend with our special person.

One day, we will get to tell them all about our journey. Until that day, your person will watch as they are in heaven next to the One (God) who created love, and He IS love.

Let's hope again, my friend, in the sorrowful and joyful times woven together.

Chapter 17

LIVING PROOF

I received a text from an old friend today. She said I am living proof one can be okay after losing someone you love and seeing my mom and I go through what we did brings her the strength to know people can overcome the pain.

Those are some of the most refreshing, affirming words someone grieving wants to hear. Because there were hundreds, no thousands, of points where I didn't think I could breathe another day. I remember texting my family and friends that I wouldn't be the same anymore and didn't know how I would handle this, and I felt dead inside. I begged everyone to pray. I became so desperate I even almost hired a person who proclaimed a healing magic…. (if you're wondering, I didn't) I didn't think I would ever get through losing my best friend-dad.

I think one difficult aspect of having a friend losing someone or about to lose a dear friend is you empathize with the suffering. You know deep down nothing will ever get them through that pain. They want an answer so much to get them over their anguish. But you know no word can bring the comfort they need.

Can You Surrender?

One of the hardest things I believe when your person's time is moments away from a final farewell is the act of surrendering. There is this fine balance between acceptance and surrender in that moment when you know and acknowledge in your mind no one can do anything else. *What do you mean he can't leave!? My dad could always leave the hospital. There was always a miracle. Give him time and more medication. Do all You got to bring him back. God, please answer my prayer, make my dad healthy again, and bring him back.*

I didn't realize then but see better now is God may not have answered my prayer the way I would've wanted because God answered my prayer of making my dad healthy. I mean, he is now the healthiest he could have ever been. My dad is walking now… running in heaven. But I wanted him here, with me, on earth.

Those words the doctor spoke have haunted me since my dad's final week. The doctor looked me in the eyes for maybe the hundredth time and said my dad would not be leaving the hospital room. As a daughter, knowing I couldn't fight and advocate for my dad anymore—the man who loved me and would have moved mountains to be there for me—brought me to my knees in an act of surrender. I remember falling into the bathroom floors at the hospital, and begging God to give my dad another miracle. Just one more miracle. Just one. As long as we dealt with my dad's situation for decades, we knew there would come a point where his body couldn't handle any more.

I Wasn't Ready

His fight wasn't over, but he was going home. I knew when that time came, we would be ready. But let me tell you, I was not ready. No one can prepare you for that moment where you have to leave the room without your person. Friend, the day my dad stayed back in that hospital room while we left was the day my heartbeat started a new rhythm, as if the rhythm skipped a beat. Leaving my dad in the room after he passed while we left was something I would never wish upon anyone. The only comfort I found that brought the beat back to my heart was knowing where my dad was and how his heart was so full and his body was new, and his life was beyond anything one can imagine.

We didn't leave my dad in the hospital after he passed because he was no longer in his body. His real body and spirit were in paradise. No, we didn't leave my dad. My dad went home. He went to what I would imagine Hawaii with tons of golden fluorescent biolumines-cence glitter flying everywhere. He was so busy catching up with all his friends and his mom in heaven; I imagine him looking down, confused about why we were even crying. *Why is my family crying, God? Don't they know I am the happiest and healthiest I've ever been, and we will all be together sooner than they can imagine?*

But do not forget this one thing, dear friends: With the Lord a day
is like a thousand years, and a thousand years are like a day.
2 Peter 3:8 NIV

There is no time in heaven, so your person in heaven knows the reunion with each other is so much closer than you can imagine. To them, they will think a day hasn't gone by in heaven without seeing you.

From Desperate to Acceptance

There come points in your life where desperation seems to be the stopping point of everything happening. You are desperate for heal-ing, desperate for change, desperate for the doctors to come in with a new prognosis, and desperate to hear the words "what a miracle."

Throughout all those desperate moments when sitting in the waiting room or next to the hospital bed, I've learned that we beg and cry out for God to show us His goodness, and when no change comes, we curse Him. We lose our self, our faith, and our hope. We create the callous in our hearts.

I continue to learn that sometimes God won't change the outcomes or circumstances in desperate moments. But over time, He will supernaturally change our hearts and prayers with the power of His love and bring hope to another aspect of what we expect. Will that person recover from cancer? Maybe not, but will you look at it with another outcome, knowing that whatever happens in the end, your person will be healed? Will the prognosis still be poor from the doctor? Most likely, yes, but will you smile knowing you have more laughs and time to spend with family now? Yes. Will you stop trying to research all the treatments and holistic routes and instead use that time praying God will be the ultimate healer?

You see, friend, desperate can turn into acceptance. You are not agreeing but accepting. Whatever it may be, your circumstances are what they are in the moment, and you have absolutely no control over what's happening. But what you have is the Source directly to heaven, a prayer away, to heal your heart and bring comforting hands to hold you through everything. Through searching for the peace and comfort only Jesus can give, I am recovering. I know seeking Him was the supernatural peace none can explain that brought moments of comfort my heart needed, and He can give you that peace too.

My purpose behind writing through my experiences is to bring living proof to you that if I could go through the most excruciating pain of grief, you, too, my friend, can and will go through similar trenches and make it out more resilient than ever.

Chapter 18

BORROWED TIME

This morning at church, our pastor shared how he would be so upset with his kids for leaving their belongings in the middle of the garage. With tears coming down his eyes, he said God reminded him there would come a day a skateboard wouldn't be laying there any longer. Then he would wish a skateboard were blocking his way. That's how quick and fast time flies. Someone can be here one day and gone the next moment.

When I look at my mom today, I am so happy to see how much she's thriving and gaining strength in her widowhood and how God provides her with so much joy and fulfillment. But, there's this sadness, knowing how every year is another year my mom is aging, which means her time is getting closer to reuniting with her husband, my dad.

Time to Accept the Truth

Instead of trying to downplay and ignore the truth, I live in and accept we are all living on borrowed time. The next hour is not promised. That's why living in the here is so crucial. Because time is so fleeting, we are breezing through this time on earth. All those small arguments and annoyances with my mom seem to fly out the window when I remember we don't know when the last time we see each other will be the last time. So, I love her every moment I have. If you haven't spoken to someone you love in a while, I encourage you to text them right now. Go visit them. Tell them how much you love them.

When our day comes that God calls us back to our real home, all the pain and suffering a loved one or we went through will all make sense. I wish I could have all the answers to our suffering. I wish I could push a button and hear God's answers through my cell phone. Answers to why all those chemo treatments ended, all those hospital visits, ambulances coming to the house, the mistreatments, the broken hearts, and all the times we questioned if God was so good, then why? The question of the century.

There will come a time, on the other side of eternity when God will lay everything in heaven out before us, and we will smile with great victory, knowing we survived all the pain and sufferings. When God reveals everything in His presence, we will have the pure bliss of seeing the truth of His grander plan laid out before us. We can live with that anticipation and truth. I don't know about you, but I am so ready and excited to race you in heaven to that layout and see everything was all worth the struggle in the end.

Before You Are Too Late

When I was growing up, a very dear friend mentored me about the work world. At a young age, I accepted a job offer from a woman who gave me the chance and opportunity of my real big girl job. I remember the time was like yesterday when we talked about life outside of work. The bond and closeness we developed created a special connection between the two of us. After almost a decade later, with times changing, we split our ways.

I heard from a family member stating my mentor friend wasn't in the healthiest condition. Throughout those months, we shared conversations over the phone with each other; we cried together; we laughed together. She even promised to help with the wedding. Seeing someone who was once so healthy decline so quick, was a trigger in my heart, reminding me how fragile life is. I got a call from a family member of hers who told me I should come see her because she wasn't looking too good. At this stage, our sweet friend was already in hospice.

On a holiday weekend, the family asked us to come see her. I remember telling my mom we needed to go visit my friend that afternoon. My mom said to wait since the next day would be the most realistic. She was right, but something inside me nudged me to go that day, no hesitation. So while I was agreeing with my mom, I got ready and dressed to go visit my mentor. My mind was saying no, but my body was like… let's go. When I was ready and dressed, I asked my mom if she was ready, and she responded, "Yup, let's go." We drove for almost five hours on a Friday during rush hour. A big shout out to the husband for driving us.

I'm glad I listened to the Holy Spirit's nudge to go. When we arrived, the nurse told us "any moment before she passes." We were thankful we visited our dear friend, even though she was in a comatose state. We got to hold her hands, listen to music, and share the good memories and all she taught me. She even squeezed gently my mom's hand while we were praying over her. We called some friends so she could hear their voice. We left soon after. The next morning, I got a call, and before listening to the message, something in me sensed sadness and peace before even answering. Our sweet girl passed away in peace. We knew with her passing that God wanted us there to say that last prayer, for her to hear the impact she made on this earth.

Imagine if we had waited until the next morning for the most realistic move. You see, friends, life doesn't have a specific timeline when time is up for us. A life could end in the next second or the next year. No one knows but God. There's no realistic time for anything. God knew all along those years before that day that we would all be together. When you have the opportunity to love on someone, do so. Don't wait. You want to know you loved all you could before it's too late.

People come into our lives for a reason, and most of that reason is to love. Hold the hand of the person who has no one, pray over a sick friend, and be that encourager. Let's not give love timelines. Let's not wait for the perfect time because there won't be one. Make that apology or things right when you need to. Lay aside the pride. Forgive frequently times seven. Tomorrow is not promised, so let's strive to love this very moment.

Chapter 19

THREE PERCENT

Navigating our lives in this crazy world is almost as if we are holding a road map called google, figuring out who we are. Why are we feeling what we are? Identity crisis seems to be on the rise, and it doesn't look like coming down the mountain soon.

Who Are You?

If we base our identity and value on decisions, who we are on relationships, and our self-worth on status... we're setting ourselves for a mock tail of depression and anxiety. Let's be honest. Living in this generation with every success and celebration posted and scrolled through our fingers can become an outlet of destruction to our mental health, but only if we allow such thinking to consume us. God created and designed us to love and to be loved. Let's remove our focus from proving or gaining our self-worth from others and start loving others as best we can by being the best version of ourselves.

Friend, you don't need to push down or forget your emotions and insecurities. You can place that urge to compete for value in the hands of someone who cares to bring serenity and peace back into your lives, Jesus.

When you go through a change, a loss, or anything altering your routine, an identity issue can become the main character. An identity issue can become an aggravation by having a lack of direction and asking yourself what to do now. With mourning, one situation or event doesn't trigger pain. Your pain can be triggered and felt at any point, anywhere.

I believe grief is this emotion with no limits or crosses the boundaries in every way. But I've learned to recognize the emotion——as something that comes with a deeper root. We must dig deep and figure out what that deeper root may be. Take the moment to letting all the control and comparisons go.

Finding peace after a life-altering event can only begin when you start with being real. I say these words all the time to myself, "in order to heal, you must be real." Your emotions may not be true. Most of the time they aren't, but what's true is the trigger and deep internal root we must bring out and ask the hard questions, "Why am I feeling this?" I can suggest one main reason is fear. God is no spirit of fear. He is quite the opposite.

The world will tell you how to grieve, where to place your identity, climb the ladder to success, have kids by a specific age, or have your retirement at an exact time. But here is the truth, my friend... only the One who created you can allow time to surface your plan.

You Are Royalty!

I can tell you this for sure... You are the daughter of a King. You are royal, no matter what others may have told you. You are breathing, which means you have a purpose. You are alive, so you have life. You have the choice today to do the hard work by letting go of which emotions spent too long in the heart, and digging internally to work on the comfort your soul desires.

Place your trust and faith in a God who loves and sees you, who wants nothing but the best for you. Even when things aren't going well, you must trust. This is almost as if I am preaching to myself, cause girl, trust me, I don't feel up for faith 97 percent of the time... but the 3 percent moments when I do... like I mean, I really do are energizing. Be the 3-percent girl. Allow the sparkle to flow back into your hearts. You got this. I'm cheering for you. Healing comes when you align your identity back in line with the One who sees and knows everything.

Chapter 20

BLOOMING

Does anyone else have a love-hate relationship with rain? When the temperature is one hundred degree in the middle of July, are you eager for rain to pour while you enjoy a warm cup of coffee? When winter comes, do you stare at the first rain with pure bliss and later end up in your room wishing for bonfire season? We aren't ever satisfied, are we?

I live in San Diego, or what most like to call "Sunny San Diego." Our winter is seventy-eight degrees. We so want to wear our warm fuzzy boots the moment the temperature hits seventy degrees with our pumpkin spice lattes. Our rain is a few minutes of drizzle that comes with heavy traffic of people who seem to have forgotten how to drive. But these last few weeks, the rainstorm was different to where the airlines canceled hundreds of flights. I'm looking outside my water-stained window with swollen eyes from having a low-key breakdown yesterday, but no one's going to know, right? Add a few inches of concealer, foundation, and contour, and boom, I am good to go.

The Beauty of Rain

But as I'm sitting here reflecting on the beauty of rain and how a cute little bird is sitting on our tree despite this storm… this cute little macho fluffy bird has been chirping and even looks like drinking the water in the sky. I was curious why my new friend was singing in the rain drizzle, so I dug into my curiosity, and I found out, "Falling rain and high humidity also add lots of water molecules to the air. That water takes space in the air, making it even less dense. So rather than fly, many birds perch and conserve energy during a storm."[2]

Then I heard Mr. Fluffy Macho sing a few tunes, so I researched that, "Rain can create changes in the environment, too, bringing worms to the surface and insects out to dry themselves. The birds may flit about grabbing these tasty morsels and chirping to let other birds know dinner is served."[3]

Sometimes, the season of what seems like the endless rain of pain we are sitting in, the dark gloomy moments, is God getting our hearts to lean into Him. Sounds so cliché, right? But the words are true. Maybe you've been in such a rush of emotions, activities, or even doing ministry but not real ministry, and God is calling you to rest and sit. Or maybe God is telling you to give your battles to Him, cry in the rain, or scream and be mad at the stabbing heartache you feel. Don't try to hustle and bustle your way through the day, fighting the winds, running away from your pain, but sit in the storm while Jesus fights your battles.

Interesting how birds even have community, calling out for each other. Being alone can cause the mind to wander to territories where we aren't meant to be alone. Grieving causes your hearts to be vulnerable. So, break bread with your sisters. Asking for help and prayers is one of the bravest things you can do, more so when going through a hard time.

The enemy will try to isolate and distort your mind with many lies when you're in this storm of grief or heartache, but like Mr.

Macho Bird… call out to your community, go get dinner, inspire yourself to get that latte with a friend. When all we see is the rain and gloom and what seems like a useless, hopeless heartache, it becomes this endless challenge. But when the rain is over, you'll see the blooming plants, which needed the storm and how the rain was a necessary chapter into the season of blossoming to become the queen you are.

Embracing the Purpose in the Storm

You see, my sweet friend, I break down and lose hope all the time. I'd be lying if I told you I see the purpose behind the pain at all times because sometimes, I doubt. I feel lost, guideless, scared, and fearful all at the same time. I fear losing another loved one. I fear rejection. I fear, I fear, and I fear. I know God is not a spirit of fear, and we must call that doubt *a lie*. I sometimes have to say aloud, "Get behind me, you lie."

Jesus created our hearts to pump, to be emotional empathic humans so desperately wanting to love and be loved. At the same time, our human nature is afraid of love, especially after a few heartbreaks. But if you trust Jesus, our Father, our creator—the one who knows every trauma hidden deep in your heart—then call out to Him in faith, believing before seeing Jesus promises to bring the hope that surpasses all understanding. A peace that none can explain.

During my dad's time in and out of hospitals, nursing homes, and sitting in the car screaming at the hospital, God provided this peace when I called out to Him. When I was done yelling and throwing my Bible across the room, I felt God see me almost as if He wanted to hear my raw anger and bitterness at what was happening. He wanted me to get to the point of true surrender and stillness to sense His comfort. God can rewire and renew your mind. He can bring a calmness in your nervous system if you pray and attune to Him on what brings the anxiety to you.

Sit in the storm, my friend. Sit in the hurt, anguish, and pain, call a friend, or go have lunch with a friend. Know this rain of pain if not forever, and through the thunder, will come a blooming season of joy. May the encouragement and promise in knowing you will recover fill you.

They Told Me Time Would Heal

When you just lose someone, one of the most common phrases others tell you is "time will heal," and while that brings a spark of light, I think those words can also bring an urgency of rush. A rush that, in time, the pain will go away. Or at least that's what I hoped. Sometimes, when you hear those words, your heart can wish that in just an x amount of time, your life would be less painful. Or you wonder why you're still feeling the pain when it's been x amount of months or even years. My pain when my dad left this earth is a drastic change from what I feel now, and it was only through time and God's love I experienced that transition.

Only time allowed me to experience the true absence of what I lost, the heaviness of the new normal, and the ache of his absence. My new normal was searching for my dad in crowded areas and trying to find any ounce of encouragement and comfort. Time was helpful because if I were to endure all that deep sorrow all at once in the beginning, I am not sure how I would have come through that tornado of emotions.

God allowing us to go through these waves is refreshing. Like the ocean, the waves come and go, and time allows the gloom to come and go. Instead of having the mindset that time will heal, think more as time will allow you to process and better manage what you feel. Time will give you the space to catch up with what your heart is feeling. Time will give you the days to relearn what this new life is to be.

Will the longing and ache still be there while going through the years? Yes. Will you find new life again? Again, yes. In time, you will learn new passions and love again. You will make new memories with great joy and cry for the lost memories. You will be grateful for the time you have with your family with you today, but you will also cry for the family that can't be here with you. The "joy and sorrow mocktail" is what I like to call it.

I miss my dad calling me all the time, asking if I was okay. Every person I see in a crowded room, I envision him standing there. Every tree I see, I envision my dad leaning against it. Years later, I still long for my dad to text me. But now, I can better understand and use my experience for a greater purpose. I can now acknowledge that absence, happiness, and sorrow intertwine. I've learned to release those intertwining emotions as I write through these pages. Time gave me that space to use the hopelessness and place my pain in these words you read.

The pain and longing will still be there, always. Imagine yourself floating on the ocean, coming so close to shore, being at peace for just a moment, and in a matter of time, the water will take you back into the waves. Only because of time can you now better prepare yourself for what to feel and how to manage the waves.

Well Done, Today

There is so much beauty and hope when we keep our perspective on the eternal. When we place our thoughts, actions, and mind to the expectation of what lays ahead of us. When going through such deep distraught, believing with faith heaven is a place of serenity, brings the only ounce of joy we can fathom. We may think as if the one way we can live again is by seeing into the future because the present brings too much pain.

I recognize throughout the messiness of trauma, heartache, and grief, I sometimes fixate my thoughts a little too much on the future. Don't assume for a second, I'm not about hopeful thinking for the future because that was my only comfort when learning to navigate my way.

But sometimes, we must bring our mind back to the present moment if we truly want to regain our peace. We must focus on loving now, seeing the person in front of you, and going outside and seeing the detailed colors of nature. We need to place the phone inside our car while we go walk outside. Take slow, deep breaths as you live and truly give your attention to who God placed in your life today.

When you lie your head on your pillow at night, you can truly hear the words He gently speaks in your heart, "well done *today,* My child." Hopeful belief for the future and the present is both comforting when we strive to have the common denominator of having hope. So, friend, be hopeful in the now and for the future. Be softer and kinder to your spirit and be here now so you can become who God designed you to be while you move forward. Did that seem like a lot of "hope" I wrote there, or was that me? If not… HOPE, HOPE, HOPE, and more HOPE.

> *His master replied, "Well done, good and faithful servant! You have been faithful with a few things; I will put you in charge of many things. Come and share your master's happiness!"*
> *Matthew 25:21*

Conclusion

ORDINARY THINGS TO CREATE EXTRAORDINARY THINGS

Friend, here we are. We arrived together at the final chapter. What a journey of reading and writing alongside with you. Please, if you haven't yet; give yourself all the love you deserve. Treat yourself out, go do what brings peace to your soul because reading a book during the hard times with all you're going through is challenging. The road you are walking through is rough, so the fact you took the time to read and learn and be intentional about your healing is something to be proud of. Agony and suffering have this gripping power, but the way you picked that up, gingerly placed the book in your hands, and read along, you deserve applause.

My hope and prayer as you have reached this final chapter is you have enjoyed just an ounce of comfort in the sacred time you set aside to recover from your anguish and distress. No matter what that healing may look like to you, the only progress one can make is owning, recognizing, and sharing their story. Your progress with your soul should thrill you because you took the energy to learn, work on, and pray through all the different difficult valleys sorrow bring. As we close our time together, I want to remind you what you received from this book will be the continuation of this life-learning journey.

Mourning doesn't just end. Heartaches don't just fade. They go, and they come back again as we live in different seasons. Some seasons are small, while others may stall your life, altering your identities. What you have read throughout this time is the hope you can prepare and apply in all areas of your future seasons. You can bring encouragement to a hurting friend. Now, you, too, can pour into other hearting hurts.

In 2013, I'll never forget a moment between my mom and me during the time when we were searching for a LTACH (Long-term acute care hospitals) for my dad, since he now depended on life-support because of his disability. One day after leaving the hospital and seeing my dad, we drove a couple miles down south to a home care. Stained carpets and bugs I've never seen crawled all over the patients' medical equipment throughout the facility. We couldn't bear the smell and sound for even a few seconds. Knowing this was a home for some patients blew my mind. We could see the quality of care for this home was poor. After my mom took a little stroll around, we went back into the car, sat for a few seconds, took one look at each other, and bawled our eyes out while holding each other. Seeing the conditions of this house plus the long road ahead for our family was overwhelming right then.

We knew our new reality and our new normal would be uncomfortable. Our tears were cries of anger, sadness, and pure despair, wishing, hoping, and praying there would be another way. We didn't know how we would ever get through and didn't think we would ever be okay. We wanted my dad to recover and go back to how things used to be. My dad stayed there for a few weeks before we could switch him closer to our home.

From then on, at every nursing facility my dad lived in, we made the most of our situations. My mom started a nursing home ministry where she held church services every Sunday for the families and residents. She started her own ministry called, "sweet dreams" where she would go to each room and tuck in the patients whose blankets were pulled down, or whose shirt was off the shoulder, and even more so the ones with no family.

We became their family. Some of my closest friends I made, who are no longer here with us today, were some residents. Most didn't remember us the next day, but we remembered them and how they impacted our lives more than us hoping to do for theirs. All the holidays for almost a decade, we spent with the residents with no family. We brought the family to them. You see, friends, did we want to go to the nursing home for all those years every day to be with my dad? Heck no. Did we have a choice? Heck no again. But did we choose to make the most out of every situation? Heck, triple yeah!

Looking back from that car moment, my mom and I have had many years now to reflect and see how much we overcame together, side by side. We share a beautiful, deep daughter and mother bond that one can never move. Character over comfort with faith grounded in the center.

I can promise life will continue to be hard, and we will never know what the next hour will bring. I can guarantee life will also bring beauty in the pain. Our special person we love can still be alive in our hearts if we share the light of love with everyone around us.

My loving, remarkable mom once said we can make "ordinary things to create extraordinary things." No matter where your life may lead you, you can bring healing and hope back again by not allowing the pain to guide you down south. But you can bring your life back up north by being you. Embrace the story of your past because you are a survivor, so allow those moments as pure opportunities to bring magical times anywhere you are. You no longer have to allow victimhood to hold you hostage because you can rise above it. That may be smiling to the family sleeping on the street corner, hugging a nursing home resident, assuring the hospital patient he is seen with value, or telling the wheelchair-bound person they have a purpose. You have the choice to make this world a better, soothing place.

We are all broken people—people in this place called earth—who need to be loved. God made us for Him. God designed us by love, for love, and to love. Grief and heartaches come with being human, but finding the balance of joy and sorrow between it all is the key to healing.

There will always be a broken aspect in my heart since the afternoon my dad went to heaven. My only source of comfort is to know I will see him again. I miss my dad, and I cry in his absence every week. But I know, one day, when I see him, he will run and carry me while hugging me like he never could before. I envision he will run fearlessly with his healthy body toward me as I run toward him with arms wide open, glancing to the side and seeing my baby Mocha Chihuahua and our pup Chanel skip alongside him. He will walk me through heaven's gates and lead me to the way of Jesus as I hear the words, "well done, My daughter, Hannah."

I'm a huge imagination girlie. I love everything imaginations represent, the curiosity—all of it. When that special day comes when I enter heaven, I imagine Jesus turning around and bringing out two jars. I ask what those jars represent. He says every tear you cried He kept recorded in this jar. I see myself curious about the other jar. I hear Jesus telling me the second jar was the tears He shed when I grieved. "Jesus Wept" (John 11:35 KJV).

As I walk toward Him, I imagine the two jars shattering, creating a river of tears floating me toward Him. Psalm 56:8 says, "You keep track of all my sorrows. You have collected all my tears in your bottle. You have recorded each one in your book" (NLT). Friends, your jar of pain is in the hands of Jesus.

I imagine that as I look around the walls in heaven as I come to Jesus, I see photos of Jesus standing alongside us at the hospital. I see Jesus sitting in my car as I drove home alone, brokenhearted with His arms around my shoulder. I see Jesus walking me down the aisle on my wedding day. I see Jesus opening the doors at the nursing home for us and wheeling my dad across the hallways. I see Jesus holding my mom's hand as she cried over my dad. I see Jesus hugging my dad as his final breaths ended. Jesus was there. Jesus is here. Jesus has and will always be with us.

I love the stillness sunsets bring across the ocean's floor. They remind me of what's coming and assure me in their special way that everything will somehow end up being okay.

You are living the new normal after loss. Please, be compassionate and kind to yourself. Life is about love and relationships. Healing is about hope. Heartbreaks are about redemption. If you haven't heard it enough in this book, you, yes, you, were made on purpose, for a purpose.

We love God by loving people. I encourage you, my friend, to hope again. Breathe again. Believe again. Heaven is real and paradise is upon us all. One day, there will be no more tears and pain. Losing our loved one is never goodbye. The legacy and love will forever pump into our hearts. The heartbreaks made you, you.

Once we step into that truth of life and allow our Father to re-mold our hearts back through our scars as we exhale, only then can we inhale the life back into our inner soul. We then realize all along, the restoration healing will come in perfect, still peace.

Love you, my new friend. We are in this together, always. My Sister in Christ for life xoxo.

– Love, from a healing heart,
Hannah Joya

Appendix 1

SCRIPTURE VERSES FOR HEALING

The next few pages are for your personal time and reflection when you want to refer back to them. When you're having one of those days, you can go back and read what Scripture promises us.

Bible Verses for Loss

Romans 14:8
If we live, we live for the Lord; and if we die, we die for the Lord. So, whether we live or die, we belong to the Lord.

Matthew 5:1-3
Now when Jesus saw the crowds, he went up on a mountainside and sat down. His disciples came to him, and he began to teach them. He said: "Blessed are the poor in spirit, for theirs is the kingdom of heaven.

2 Corinthians 4:17-18
For our light and momentary troubles are achieving for us an eternal glory that far outweighs them all. So we fix our eyes not on what is seen, but on what is unseen, since what is seen is temporary, but what is unseen is eternal.

Psalm 73:26
My flesh and my heart may fail, but God is the strength of my heart and my portion forever.

Comforting Scriptures for Death

1 Corinthians 15:42-44
So will it be with the resurrection of the dead. The body that is sown is perishable, it is raised imperishable; it is sown in dishonor, it is raised in glory; it is sown in weakness, it is raised in power; and it is sown a natural body, it is raised a spiritual body. If there is a natural body, there is also a spiritual body.

John 11:25-26
Jesus said to her, "I am the resurrection and the life. The one who believes in me will live, even though they die; and whoever lives by believing in me will never die. Do you believe this?"

2 Corinthians 5:8
We are confident, I say, and would prefer to be away from the body and at home with the Lord.

When the Grief and Heartaches Are Too Heavy

Revelation 21:4
He will wipe every tear from their eyes. There will be no more death or mourning or crying or pain, for the old order of things has passed away.

Psalm 34:18
The LORD is close to the brokenhearted and saves those who are crushed in spirit.

Psalm 147:3
He heals the brokenhearted and binds up their wounds.

Joshua 1:9
Have I not commanded you? Be strong and courageous. Do not be afraid; do not be discouraged, for the LORD your God will be with you wherever you go.

Romans 8:28
And we know that in all things God works for the good of those who love him, who have been called according to his purpose.

Matthew 5:4
Blessed are those who mourn, for they will be comforted.

1 Thessalonians 4:13-14
Brothers and sisters, we do not want you to be uninformed about those who sleep in death, so that you do not grieve like the rest of mankind, who have no hope. For we believe that Jesus died and rose again, and so we believe that God will bring with Jesus those who have fallen asleep in him.

1 Thessalonians 4:17-18
After that, we who are still alive and are left will be caught up together with them in the clouds to meet the Lord in the air. And so we will be with the Lord forever. Therefore encourage one another with these words.

John 16:22 (NASB95)
Therefore you too have grief now; but I will see you again, and your heart will rejoice, and no one will take your joy away from you.

Psalm 9:9 (NASB95)
The LORD also will be a stronghold for the oppressed, A stronghold in times of trouble.

Psalm 46:1 (KJV)
God is our refuge and strength, a very present help in trouble.

Revelation 14:13
Then I heard a voice from heaven say, "Write this: Blessed are the dead who die in the Lord from now on." "Yes," says the Spirit, "they will rest from their labor, for their deeds will follow them."

John 14:1-2
Do not let your hearts be troubled. You believe in God; believe also in me. My Father's house has many rooms; if that were not so, would I have told you that I am going there to prepare a place for you?

1 John 3:2
Dear friends, now we are children of God, and what we will be has not yet been made known. But we know that when Christ appears, we shall be like him, for we shall see him as he is.

Romans 8:18 (ESV)
For I consider that the sufferings of this present time are not worth comparing with the glory that is to be revealed to us.

Appendix 2

A GUIDELINE OF QUESTIONS TO HELP YOU FIND HOPE AGAIN

I believe journaling is such a healthy habit for healing. I've been journaling since I was a little girl and can say writing is such a beautiful outlet on expressing your inner emotions. I hoped to create the time and encouragement for you to start if you haven't yet. Below are some kick-starter questions to get your heart going.

Whether morning, afternoon, or evening, you can decide when's best for your soul to share your thoughts on paper.

- What were some of your special person's favorite things to do?
- What were some moments you treasured together?
- How can you continue their legacy? What can you do to make them smile if they were here with you today?
- What words would you share to your younger self enduring a heartbreak?
- What is one life lesson you carry today after going through a heartbreak?

- What are some dreams you have for your future self that bring a sense of peace?
- When you contemplate peace, what do you think of?
- When you think of healing, what comes to mind?

Thank you for taking the time and energy into reading my book!

If you enjoyed reading this book and would like to read along and learn more about my early stages of grief and more in-depth of my family's life, then my first book, *Never Goodbye* #girldad is for you. You can find a copy in bookstores and online, etc.

Excerpt from
Never Goodbye

Because you are so awesome,
will include a chapter of *Never Goodbye* just for you 😊.

WHAT IS Life?

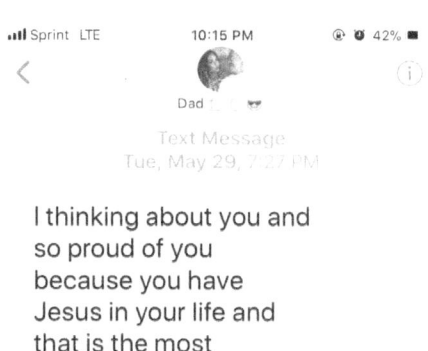

I thinking about you and so proud of you because you have Jesus in your life and that is the most important thing love you

Remember count your blessing

Remember that Jesus love you OK

Put your trust in him and not in your emotions

T hat was the last text I received from my dad before he passed; before Heaven received the best gift that life could have given me. That day, I lost my hero, my best friend, my iron man. That day, I lost all faith in existence.

Why live anymore? How could I continue with my life if he was my life? Death and grief do something to you; that was a day I will never forget. The day I held his hand to my face, expecting his fingers to be warm reassurance, but instead turning ice cold within seconds. The day I saw his body turn from white to blue. I couldn't even look at my dad's face when he was taking his final breaths because I was terrified to see what was happening. That day, I ran out of tears. That day, I lost me. That day, I cursed God. Two people died that late afternoon on June 13, 2018, my dad and me. Here today; gone tomorrow. The enemy used that day to break me, but in the end, you'll see God used the circumstances to make me. Pain gives you two choices: to make or break you. You get to decide.

On that day, I watched my dad enter Heaven's gates right before my eyes and through that, I learned how to completely surrender. What is life?

You may or may not have lost someone. Maybe your story sounds similar to mine. Maybe our grief, losses or heartaches in these next chapters are completely opposite or perfect reflections of each other. Whatever your story is, we most likely have one thing in common; pain. Grief, pain and heartache don't discriminate. Whether you're twenty-seven or forty-seven, heck even eighty-seven, pain is pain. No matter if you went through a tragic accident and lost someone in five minutes or you lost someone over a span of five years, loss is loss; the hurt is the same across all fronts. Don't compare traumas because the time hasn't been as long as someone else's. Pain isn't a competition, and if grief recovery was a race, I certainly wouldn't want to be the winner. We all deserve recovery and support. The common denominator with everyone's story on loss, is pain.

I wasn't ready; he wasn't ready. No one is ever really ready for death. In this book, you will encounter and be a witness to my stories of pain, grief, depression, anxiety, loss and heart break I endured throughout my life. Without God's pursuing love, I would not have gotten through any of my pain and struggles. With God, I could build resilience and see the lesson behind the struggle.

Pastor Rick Warren states there are six stages to grief: shock, sorrow, struggle, surrender, sanctification and service. I lived in shock, depression, PTSD, and denial after my dad's passing for one year straight; every single day and night. Not until later on I could trudge through the struggle. What I thought was the struggle initially, wasn't even close. At twenty-seven years old, losing my best friend, my dad, was the only thing I could focus on. As a family, we were challenged to get through all that.

Are you in a season of perpetual negativity or think your whole life is a broken record of sadness? Is crying yourself to sleep your new normal because you don't see the joy in life and accepting numbness is your new routine? Depression is now your reality. Anxiety is everywhere you go. Waking up with dread in your heart knowing you somehow have to muster energy for the day standing before you. Wishing a miracle would appear. Questioning your existence. You wonder, what really is life? Is your life worth living? What is my purpose? If you've had any of those things or thoughts, you've picked up the right book, my new friend.

The encouragement I have for you now, wherever you are, at this very moment remember this right here, right now, is not the final chapter. The impossible will become possible. You will finish this book, you will take something from this moment, and you will choose joy over sorrow. This is God's promise to us—He is close to those who are brokenhearted. I know what self-isolation, emptiness, and enduring true tragedy feels like.

While we journey through this book together, hold dear to your heart that your life has a purpose. No pain goes without purpose. You will forge through this tunnel and come out on the other side much stronger than you could've imagined. I will reignite the resilience God made ready for you, my new friend. I hope you don't mind me calling you "friend" throughout this book. You know being vulnerable and writing my story wasn't easy, but through prayer, God made clear to me that someone—maybe you—needed to hear my story. A story of a girl who overcame obstacles the enemy carefully placed in her path, forcing her to dig deep into her soul to discover the tenacity for life through God. These words I write won't bring my dad back, but they did bring me healing in the process. Not only are you suffering grief, heartache or loss, but I am as well. We are en route together, blooming in a new season of healing and growth. I'll say these words again for the people in the back, you are NOT alone!

I hope you accept my invitation of friendship, which may come as a surprise to you, but since friends tell each other secrets… People called me "weird" my entire life. People would always say I was too outgoing, talkative, or hyper. They would say, "No one will want to be friends with you," so I tried to hide my personality.

In fourth grade students teased me about my ethnicity. Being Korean, Filipino, and Spanish, I would constantly get asked why my eyes were so small or why my face was so flat. Kids used to compare my face to a plate and make fun of the Asian snacks I would have at school. The teasing made me fearful no one would want to be friends with the "weirdo" so I ate my packed lunch of sushi and lumpia in the bathroom stall, alone.

I was never insecure about my dad's disability. When I stopped caring what other people thought of me and decided to only care about what God saw in me, I really gained confidence and realized my self-worth. The bondage of insecurity chaining me down no longer kept a stronghold on my authentic self. God created us to be unique and special, so be you. Be the "you" God designed you to be. I'm most definitely an extrovert, but at the same time, I enjoy being alone. I love reading and writing by my favorite candle, listening to relaxing, soft tunes while sipping on a smooth cup of coffee. We are all special in our own way; don't let society or anyone tell you otherwise.

If you still allow lies to rear their ugly face in your mind, God has the power to remove them. Stay strong, stand your ground, and do not allow those lies to have power over your life, let God. So now that you know a bit more about me, and you will learn quite a bit more as you read on, I think I can safely say we are now officially friends.

Throughout this book, I will share with you my raw organic truth; the life-transforming personal stories brought on through much pain and grief. Pain that became PTSD and never seemed to end. Pain that appeared to be my final destiny.

I was born to a dad who was a quadriplegic from the neck down. He had CIDP/GBS (Chronic inflammatory demyelinating polyneuropathy/Guillain-Barre syndrome) disease, a chronic illness, which created endless struggles in both my family life and personal life. The only vision of my dad, the only version I ever knew, was of him confined to a wheelchair. I never had the privilege of seeing him walk, run, swim, or dance, but those challenges didn't stop me from living life to the fullest for my dad and for myself. For so long I was heartbroken, abused, betrayed, cheated on dozens of times in relationships and my dreams were swept away by rejection, after rejection. Despair was my middle name.

When my dad passed away in 2018, I thought that was my final chapter—end of story. I didn't realize his death was the beginning of a new life. Like a gemstone refined through tremendous pressure and heat, my new life took shape. God won't get you over your pain. He'll get you through what you are dealing with. By sharing my pain, I hope you realize you can and will overcome difficulties, challenges, mountains, and fires. I'll tell you how overcoming pain to climb that mountain, to survive the trenches, and rise above what most would view as hopeless is possible. Speaking truth with beauty beyond the ashes, I'll gently guide you back to God's love, who promises hope and a future, even when we don't believe the promise is for us.

My mom's first child, my brother Mark, got to witness my dad go from a strong healthy person to being paralyzed from the neck down. Amidst this heart wrenching transition, my brother was truly a gift to my parents, which I'll speak more in depth about later on in the book. Twelve years after my brother, I was born into the world. My mom told people how I was such a blessing of laughter. My dad was so depressed, especially during the early stages of his illness, all he needed sometimes was to laugh. She would always say God knew what he was doing by giving my dad a daughter at that exact time. Lord knows how many emotions surface when a girl is born into the family. Daughters have this special power in raising a dad's blood pressure and invoking a protective mannerism that no "man" can break without permission. But in all seriousness, the extraordinary bond between a solid father-daughter relationship is unbreakable. Being a dad is the most important role a man can have in his daughter's life. #GirlDad—the special loving bond between a dad and daughter that will live on forever.

The relationship between your parents is a different bond, one that can serve as an example for honest love, if that describes your parent's relationship. As a young girl, I witnessed how my mom cared for my dad. She did all the tasks most of us take for granted. I watched her feed him, brush his hair, change his clothes, and carry him to the car—trivial and routine things for most, but caregiving for your partner is a labor of love and is no easy endeavor. When my dad needed to use the restroom at any time of the day, my mom would have to rush home and carry him from his wheelchair to his commode, wipe him, and make sure he was cleaned up before returning him to his wheelchair.

Any person could perceive that kind of love as degrading or dehumanizing, but never for my dad. He saw her actions as unconditional love. He never allowed those unique situations to damage his soul. Every morning and evening my brother and mom would stretch my dad's extremities which increased circulation in his body. We also used a stand-up machine they would strap him into so he could feel the sensation of standing again, even if only for thirty minutes.

CIDP/GBS caused him to be in pain 24/7. My dad would describe this as the tingling sensation you get when your arm or foot fell asleep, except it was all over his body, all the time. I remember pinching my dad's arm and him reacting minutes later. Sitting in the living room and watching TV as a young girl, I recall my mom transferring my dad from the shower to their bedroom, water dripping everywhere, the dogs following close behind licking up each water droplet, and my dad glancing over at me while laughing. My mom was my dad's angel, my brother and I were my dad's little angels, and now my dad is our angel; our guardian angel. Our lives should surround acts of service because that's what God calls us to do. We are here to serve, not to be served.

What makes you happy? Genuinely happy? When we think of being happy, we usually think about getting things for ourselves such as status, fame, and fortune. When we take the focus off ourselves and focus on others, it allows us to see beyond what we think we might need. It allows us to see what God desires for our true happiness. The more we serve and the more we love, the more we will be blessed with genuine joy.

If you're devoid of this joy, hopeless, discouraged, or depressed, or whatever season you may be in where you may believe God forgot you—I'm so thankful you grabbed this book to read. By the last chapter, you'll have a solid perspective on the healing power of God. You'll know how to embrace joy in the messiness of the unknown because in reality, life is all a mystery with a little thrill. But behind the unknown mystery is when God's loving hand works miracles and his true plan for you takes form. So, my prayer and hope is that through this new journey of healing you're entering in, you will embrace the revival of God's refreshing love. If I can get through my darkest days, my friend, you can too. The book cover is a real-life image of me holding my dad's hand one last time at the hospital. The last promise I made to my dad was that I would never let his story of faith and resilience go untold. I promised to never let his pain go without purpose. Almost two years later, the promise I made became a reality. You're reading this promise now.

Buckle up, friend, the season of vibrant, flourishing healing has begun.

"For I know the plans I have for you," declares the Lord, "plans to prosper you and not to harm you, plans to give you hope and a future." (Jeremiah 29:11 NIV)

So, let's do this journey of life together my friend, the best is yet to come.

About the Author

Hannah Joya is a writer, speaker, social media influencer, model, and, most importantly, a people and animal lover living in California. You most likely will catch her at the beach watching the sunset with her dogs if she isn't eating her mom's home-cooked meals or writing. Hannah's life mission stemmed from the grief of losing her father, allowing her to see people despite disabilities and loss. Hannah is the author of the best-selling *Never Goodbye #girldad* book and uses her words and inspiration to provide hope in people's grief.

Stay Connected on social media and don't be a stranger and say hi:

Instagram: hannahmariejoya
Tiktok: hannahjoya56
Facebook: Hannah Joya Smith

Endnotes

1   "How to Identify Emotional Triggers in 3 Steps," Ridgeview Hospital, Accessed July 2, 2023, https://ridgeviewhospital.net/how-to-identify-emotional-triggers-in-3-steps/#:~:text=Emotional%20triggers%2C%20also%20called%20mental,trigger%20would%20logically%20call%20for.
2   Birdnote, "Why Do Birds Avoid Flying in the Rain?" Audobon from a podcast of July 10, 2017. https://www.audubon.org/news/why-do-birds-avoid-flying-rain
3   Joan Morris, "Why Do Birds Sing after a Rain?" The Mercury News, August 11, 2016, https://www.mercurynews.com/2015/12/30/why-do-birds-sing-after-a-rain/

www.ingramcontent.com/pod-product-compliance
Lightning Source LLC
Chambersburg PA
CBHW030308130626
46549CB00002B/758